Miriam's Well

Also by Alice Bach and J. Cheryl Exum

Moses' Ark: Stories from the Bible

MIRIAM'S WELL

Stories About Women in the Bible

Alice Bach and J. Cheryl Exum

*With a frontispiece and decorations
by Leo and Diane Dillon*

Delacorte Press § New York

Published by Delacorte Press
Bantam Doubleday Dell Publishing Group, Inc.
666 Fifth Avenue/New York, New York 10103

Library of Congress Cataloging in Publication Data

Bach, Alice.
  Miriam's well : stories about women in the Bible
by Alice Bach and J. Cheryl Exum :
illustrated by Leo and Diane Dillon.
      p.   cm.
  Summary: A retelling of Old Testament stories
focusing on women including Naomi and Ruth,
Miriam, Hagar, Judith, Esther, and others.
  Includes bibliographical references.
  ISBN 0-385-30435-8
  1. Bible stories, English—O.T. 2. Women in the Bible—
Juvenile literature. [1. Bible stories—O.T. 2. Women
in the Bible.] I. Exum, J. Cheryl. II. Dillon, Leo, ill.
III. Dillon, Diane, ill. IV. Title.
BS551.2.B23 1991
90-48099   221.9′22′082—dc20   CIP   AC

Manufactured in the United States of America
November 1991
10 9 8 7 6 5 4 3 2 1

*We are grateful to
Professor Sara Japhet
of the Hebrew University of
Jerusalem for her gracious criticism
and helpful suggestions.*

For Kassie Temple,
who shines the light when I am in shadow,
and for Jacob Stuart Gilbert,
a shining light, a brand-new star

(a . b .)

For friends in the Department of Theology
at Boston College, in gratitude

(j . c . e .)

Contents

Introduction

Most of the Bible's stories center on men. Women, if they appear at all, are minor characters. Sometimes women become the focus of attention for a brief moment in a man's story; for example, the matriarchs Sarah, Rebekah, Leah, and Rachel appear at key points in the patriarchal sagas to assure that God's promises are passed on to the rightful male heir. Other times women appear on the scene only to disappear from the story after they have served their purpose. In the story of David's rise to the throne, the wise and eloquent Abigail steps in to prevent David from committing a sin that would leave him tainted with bloodguilt; though she becomes one of David's wives, we hardly hear of her again. Miriam, who lends her name to the title of our book, has no story in the sense of a narrative that focuses on her. Her story has to be woven together from scattered fragments in Exodus and Numbers. Thus we introduce a young girl, Dinah, as the narrator of Miriam's story in order to supply background information and give the story continuity.

In telling the stories of biblical women we have tried to give the women a voice where the Bible often relegates them to silence, to tell the stories from their point of view. Since the Bible gives us so little information about many of these women, we have added details to their stories from what we know about customs and society in ancient times. Sometimes we supplement one biblical story with information gleaned from other parts of the Bible; lament psalms appear in the story of Hagar, verses from the Song of Songs express Michal's love for her husband David, and Abigail knows the wisdom of Proverbs. Gaps in the text are not unique to the stories of women; they are typical of biblical narrative in particular and of storytelling in general.

Rabbinic materials proved especially useful in filling gaps with delightful anecdotes. In Jewish tradition, *aggadah* or midrash refers to the collection of stories, legends, fables, myths, and traditions about the Bible or biblical characters. Some of the midrashic collections are much older than the time in which they were written, for they were stories that had been told orally from parents to children, preached in the synagogues by the rabbis, and taught as ethical principles for human behavior. Reading the midrash can enrich the biblical stories as well as cast light upon the political, economic, and social conditions of ancient times. Sometimes the same midrash is found in different collections, indicating its wide familiarity in early Jewish communities. We have used material from two great midrashic collections on the Pentateuch (Genesis, Exodus, Leviticus, Numbers, and Deuteronomy) as well as the midrashic collections for the books of Esther and Ruth. We have blended the aggadic material into the stories we have retold in order to fill out the characters who have been fragmented in the biblical account. It is interesting that the midrashim often complete stories of women, as though answering the questions of generations of children asking, "What happened to Miriam? Why did Sarah laugh?"

The exceptions to our observations about women as minor characters are the three books about women that bear their names, Ruth, Esther, and Judith. Since women are the heroes of these books, we have followed the biblical story, adding details to expand upon what the biblical writers wrote. In the case of the book of Ruth, we call our story "Naomi and Ruth," since the story is as much Naomi's story as it is Ruth's. Though not included in Jewish and Protestant Bibles, the book of Judith was part of the Septuagint, the early Greek translation of the Hebrew Bible. Although the biblical story is told by an omniscient narrator, we have allowed Judith to tell her own exciting story. First-person narrative is not unknown in the Bible: portions of the books of Ezra and Nehemiah use this convention.

In contrast to our stories of Naomi and Ruth, Esther, and Judith, which follow the biblical accounts, "A Mosaic for Miriam" records biblical references to women too brief or incomplete to form independent stories. How might Job's wife have responded to the calamities that befell her husband? we wondered. What compulsion might Lot's wife have felt to look back one last time at her former home? In our mosaic we try to supply some possible solutions. The mosaic also includes the stories of two infamous foreign women, Delilah and Jezebel. What if they, and not the biblical writers, had been permitted to tell their own stories?

As in *Moses' Ark* we tell thirteen stories, for the thirteen children of Jacob. In Jewish tradition, thirteen is a sacred number. There are, for example, thirteen attributes of God in the Talmud. Thirteen is also the age for a person's acceptance into the community of Israel, the Bar or Bas Mitzvah. Our selection of stories shows the range and variety of roles open to women in biblical times. They span a long period of time, from the patriarchal period (considered to be 2000–1500 B.C.E.) to the Hellenistic period (300 B.C.E. to 70 C.E.). Obviously the position of women and the opportunities open to them changed over so great an expanse of time.

Although the Bible most often portrays women in the roles of wife and mother, women can be found occupying a range of leadership roles usually thought the exclusive domain of men in the Bible. There were women prophets: Deborah in the book of Judges; Huldah, whose story appears in our mosaic; Noadiah in the book of Nehemiah; and an unnamed prophet in the book of Isaiah. Miriam is also called a prophet, though the term was probably applied to her in later times. There are a few notable queens. Besides the infamous Queen Jezebel, who ruled Israel with her husband Ahab, we find Jezebel's daughter Athaliah ruling alone over the Southern Kingdom of Judah for a period of six years. In addition, in Judah the position of queen mother seems to have been an important one. By the time the population lived in towns, as well as in rural areas of the surrounding hill country, women were artisans and spent more times at the crafts of weaving, pottery, and jewelry making.

Even though there is much we do not know about women in biblical times, archaeological studies can supplement the literary evidence to give us a fuller picture. In the earliest Israelite society both women and men worked diligently all day to provide food for their families. The Bible tells us that Rachel was tending her father's flocks when she met Jacob. The woman in the Song of Songs is a shepherd, and Moses meets his future wife while she is tending her father's flock with her sisters. Women not only were in charge of the cooking and managing the household for their families but also had other important skills, such as the spinning of yarn and weaving of cloth, and the making of pottery and tools. They probably also brewed beer, made soap, and dyed cloth.

While women in the time of the matriarchs lived in tents, houses were common by the time of the Judges (1200–1000 B.C.E.). Archaeological evidence indicates that these houses were usually small two-story rectangular structures with two to four rooms. The family lived in the second story and the ground floor served as a barn, stabling the family's livestock, sheep, goats, cows, donkeys, and even camels!

In monarchic times a wealthy woman like Abigail had many responsibilities in managing the large estate of her husband. A woman of this class may also have acted as a merchant, selling the cloth of blue and purple and scarlet that she had woven; such a picture of the industrious wife is given in the book of Proverbs. One can imagine Abigail sitting in her room, the spindle flying through her deft fingers. A role model for others of her class, and for her servants, she never tasted of the bread of idleness.

Like Abigail, Judith was in charge of a large estate. She is portrayed as a Jewish widow who served as a role model for all Israelites in her temperance, generosity to the poor, and, of course, in her great courage. Esther, who became the queen of Babylon in the novella that carries her name, lived a life very different from the biblical women who toiled beside their husbands in the fields. Imagine spending an entire year being made beautiful enough for one night with a king!

While they were very young, both girls and boys were raised primarily by their mothers. As they grew older, daughters received their education from their mothers. Girls were also taught the tasks of household management, while boys learned from their fathers tasks of the field, clearing the land, and digging cisterns. Children were probably taught to read by their parents; there is no evidence that schools existed before the Hellenistic period (from the fourth century B.C.E. until the first century C.E.). Parental authority over children was also carried into the adult years in the Israelite household, which contained several generations. As Proverbs warns the young person, "Hear your father's instruction and reject not your mother's teaching." Thus the influence of mothers extended throughout the life of the children, and women held a central role in the wisdom tradition in Israel.

We have omitted from our collection stories in which there is violence committed against women, although the biblical narrators did record several rapes and other startling acts of cruelty and brutality. We preferred to retell stories where we could share women's dreams rather than their nightmares, stories in which women played positive roles, in which they were leaders, not victims, and in which their deeds advanced the story of Israel.

Miriam's Well

Sarah and the Promise

"*Go from your land and your kinspeople,*
Go from the house of your ancestors
To the land that I will show you.
I will make you a great nation.
I will bless you and magnify your name
And you will be a blessing.
I shall bless those who bless you,
And those who slight you I shall curse.
Through you all the peoples of the earth will be blessed."

Abraham hid his face with his robe and waited for God to
tell him more. Time seemed to stand still. Abraham heard

nothing but the cicadas in the tall grasses. He waited but God said nothing more.

Abraham got to his feet and went slowly home, the promises of God echoing in his ears. When he reached his house, Sarah, his wife, was carding sheepswool yarn in the courtyard.

When she saw Abraham standing before her, Sarah put down her work. "What is wrong with you, my husband? You are pale and frightened."

"I have something of great importance to tell you," he said, his voice trembling. "God spoke to me in the field. God told me that we must leave this place, we must leave our kin and go away from here."

"Leave Haran?" Sarah asked. "Why does God want us to do that?"

"God will show us a new land and will make of us a great nation." There was wonder in Abraham's voice, as though he was not quite certain of the meaning of the words he spoke.

"If it is God's will, then we can leave Haran," Sarah said calmly. "We traveled here from Ur of the Chaldeans, with your father Terah and your nephew Lot. We left all that we knew and came to this place. It was foreign to us then and now it is our home. We can make another journey."

"But to leave our relatives, and to leave everything familiar!" Abraham looked into his wife's large dark eyes. "But you are right. What God has commanded we will do."

"We must take your nephew Lot," she said, rolling up her yarn and placing it in a large bag made of carpet. "He has been like a son to us ever since his father died."

"Surely the Lord will allow us to take Lot since we have no children of our own. If we are to be a great nation, then Lot will share in our good fortune."

Three days later Sarah and Abraham rose early in the morning and packed the donkeys with saddlebags. He hid small pouches filled with pieces of silver between bolts of Sarah's cloth in a long wooden box. The servants hurried back and forth loading provisions for the long journey. They piled pottery, large cooking pots, bronze jugs, and household utensils onto the waiting donkeys. Abraham's herdsmen gathered his share of the flocks and herds and brought them to the departure site. Sarah took her place in a cart drawn by a team of oxen. In her arms she cradled a silver goblet. She thought of the day she had left her father's house to be married to Abraham, never to live among her brothers and sisters again. From the time she had been a small girl, her mother had taught her that she would grow up to live in her husband's world. The familiar hills and the tamarisk tree under which she played as a child would not be places her own children would know.

By the time the sun was high in the sky, the group had already begun its trek to the south. To the land of Canaan, an unfamiliar place.

They had been traveling for many days and still the Lord had not spoken. Lot and Abraham helped the herdsmen water the flocks. The ground in Canaan was dry as dust, and the water in the streams was running low. There had been no rainfall and the earth blistered in the heat. After hot, sun-baked days Sarah and her servants prepared the evening meals. Sarah looked up at the starry sky at night and wondered why the Lord had chosen this place to give them.

More days passed. They traveled on to a place called Shechem, where they pitched their tents and Abraham built an altar of stones to God. There God spoke to Abraham, "I shall give this land to your descendants." When Sarah heard what God had said, she was puzzled. "We have no children," she thought to herself. "And God has promised this land to our descendants."

As they continued their journey toward the south, Abraham and some of his servants tried to trade goods to the Canaanites in exchange for food, since the provisions they had brought from Haran were now quite low. The famine in the land of Canaan was so severe that Abraham decided they should travel farther south to Egypt. "There's plenty of food in Egypt, where the land is watered by the Nile," he assured Sarah.

As they were about to enter the land of Egypt, Abraham said to Sarah, "While we are in the land of Egypt, I want you to pretend that you and I are sister and brother, not wife and husband. You are so beautiful, I am afraid an Egyptian will want you for his wife. When he finds out you are married to me, he'll kill me so he can have you for himself."

"I will do as you say." Sarah lowered her eyes. During the night she thought of the hardship that lay ahead. The next day, when they could see the border of Egypt in the distance, Sarah said to Abraham, "Perhaps I could hide in the long box, the one beside me here in the cart. Then the Egyptians will not see me at all."

"It is worth a try," Abraham agreed. "Perhaps they will not be interested in the dusty old box of a simple traveler."

Lot crossed over first, with the herdsmen and the flocks. While the guards were occupied with other members of the group, Sarah climbed into the long box in the cart. Abraham piled a few pieces of cloth on top of her and locked the lid securely. Then he drove the oxen toward the guards' station.

"What is in that box?" the border guard demanded.

"Just garments," Abraham replied.

"Soft linen garments? You shall pay the tax on soft linen garments."

"That is fine, the tax on soft linen garments." Abraham took a few pieces of silver from the pouch inside his robe.

"Wait—we think there is fine silk cloth inside this box.

We shall charge you the tax for silk cloth!" The guard smiled nastily.

"Silk cloth is fine." Abraham pulled the pouch of silver from his robe.

The guard rested his hand on top of the box. "On the other hand, I suspect there are precious gems in this box. You shall pay the tax on precious gems."

"Precious gems are fine." Abraham pulled another pouch of silver from his robe.

"Open this box!" demanded the guard. "We must see what is so precious."

When the guards pulled aside the cloth covering Sarah, they exclaimed, "A woman! A beautiful woman far more precious than gems, indeed! This woman is fit for the pharaoh! We shall take her to him."

Abraham had tears in his eyes as the guards took his wife Sarah to the palace of the pharaoh.

Sarah remained in the house of Pharaoh until God came to the ruler of Egypt in a dream, and warned him that Sarah was the wife of another man. In the morning, shaken by the divine message, Pharaoh ordered that Sarah be brought to him.

"Why have you deceived me! Your God told me in a dream that you are married. Who is your husband? Is he within these palace walls?"

"We did not tell you because we feared for Abraham's life," she replied timidly. "I am sorry for the deception."

When Abraham was brought before the pharaoh, he bowed his head to the ground. His tongue was too thick with fear to utter a word of apology.

The pharaoh stepped forward. The hem of his robe brushed Abraham's cheek. "I honor a God who has the power to enter the dreams of the pharaoh of Egypt. And I return to you this beautiful woman, your wife. Honor her from this day forth, and I shall honor your God.

When you leave my kingdom, I shall give you flocks and oxen, donkeys, camels, silver and gold, and male and female servants.''

Abraham arose and said to the pharaoh, "You do me much honor by honoring my God.''

"When you return to Canaan, you must take my precious daughter Hagar," proclaimed the pharaoh. He turned to Sarah. "I am sending my daughter with you because of the miracles your God performed on your behalf. It is better that my daughter be a handmaid in such a house than a princess in another house.''

Abraham, Sarah, Lot, and all those who had gone with them to Egypt returned to the land of Canaan and settled there. Abraham and Lot had both grown very wealthy. They each had tents and flocks and herds spread out as far as the eye could see. The herdsmen of the cattle began to quarrel. The servants bickered. Abraham and Lot found themselves marking their flocks, separating their ewe lambs. Tensions grew between the two groups. "This well is ours," cried Abraham's herdsmen. "Our cattle must also have water," demanded Lot's herdsmen, driving their herds through Abraham's fields.

"Such strife between relatives is not good," Abraham told Lot one day. "There is plenty of land, for God has prospered us both. Let us divide the land between us so that our families may live in harmony. If you take the land to the left, then I will take the right. Or if you prefer the land to the right, then I will take the left.''

"I will take the Jordan valley because it is well watered, like the garden of Eden." Lot looked out over the rolling hills to the east. "May you continue to prosper," he told his uncle. Then with his family, flocks, and servants he moved his tents to Sodom.

Abraham and Sarah continued to live in the land of Canaan. Their flocks increased, and their herds multiplied. The goats gave much milk. But Sarah did not have children. Not long after Lot had separated from Sarah and Abraham, God spoke to Abraham:

"Lift up your eyes, and look from the place where you are
To the north and to the south, to the east and to the west.
For all the land that you see
I will give to you and to your descendants forever.
I will make your descendants like the dust of the earth;
if you can count the dust of the earth,
then you can also count your descendants.
Can the stars of the heavens be numbered?
That is how numerous your descendants will be.
Stride the length and breadth of the land,
for I shall give it all to you."

Abraham did as the Lord told him. He and Sarah and Hagar, their handmaid, and their servants and flocks and herds moved their tents to Hebron, where they dwelt by the oaks of Mamre. There Abraham built an altar to God.

It was springtime, and the ewes bore lambs and the goats their kids. But Sarah still bore no children. She thought of God's promise to make their descendants as numerous as the dust of the earth. So Sarah went to Abraham and told him that he must have a child with Hagar, her servant. "Then I shall obtain children through her, and God's promise to make our children as numerous as the stars in the heavens will be realized." Abraham did as Sarah told him.

When Hagar became pregnant, she refused to work. She lay in the sunshine and said loudly for all to hear, "I am to bear a child to Abraham, for it is natural for a woman to bear a child."

When Sarah heard what Hagar had said, she was very angry. She pushed aside the tent flap and demanded that her husband get rid of the sly little maidservant.

Abraham shook his head. "She is your servant; you do whatever you want with her."

Sarah stormed out of the tent and went to where Hagar was sitting with some of the other servants. One of the young women was braiding flowers through Hagar's hair. "Get up from there. Just as the ewes run through pasture-land while they are about to bear their young, so you can do your work. Get up! Get up!" she cried.

The other servants fled to the far side of the camp. Sarah picked up a shepherd's crook and waved it at Hagar. "Get out of my sight!" The younger woman jumped to her feet and ran from her mistress.

Hagar was not seen for several days. Sarah thought of God's promise and wondered if Hagar would return. On the third day, while she was watering the baby lambs, a shadow fell across the lambs' woolly backs. Sarah looked up and saw her servant Hagar standing before her. "I will water the lambs," she told her mistress. Without a word Sarah handed her the pitcher.

When Hagar gave birth to a son, Abraham named him Ishmael. Abraham's family continued to prosper. Abraham hired more herdsmen and traded with the caravans that passed through Canaan. Sarah sat with the young boy Ishmael and told him stories in the fading afternoon sun. At night she sang him lullabies and stayed with him until he fell asleep.

One afternoon in the heat of the day while Abraham sat at the door of the tent with the boy playing nearby, three men suddenly appeared. Abraham was astonished to see strangers wearing fine garments traveling without camels or servants. He got up and greeted them with excitement. "You must sojourn with us awhile. Sit here in the shade of a tree, while I bring you food and drink to refresh yourselves. You must be tired, although you do not wear the weariness of your long desert travel."

Abraham rushed inside the tent and told Sarah to prepare food for their guests. "Make ready quickly three measures of fine meal, knead it, and make cakes."

"After all these years, old man, shall you tell me how to make bread?" Sarah laughed.

Abraham hurried out to the herd, selected a calf, and had a servant prepare it for the honored guests. Then he took curds and milk and the calf that had been prepared and set it before the three men.

While they were eating their meal, one of the men looked up and spoke to Abraham. "Where is Sarah, your wife?"

"She is in the tent."

Ishmael came over and ate a bit of meat that his father offered to him.

The man motioned with his hand toward the tent. "By next spring, she will have a son of her own."

Sarah was listening at the door of the tent. When she heard the stranger's words, she laughed. "Now that I am old, and my husband is old, how could I know such pleasure?"

"Was that Sarah who laughed?" the stranger asked.

"I did not hear her laugh," Abraham responded nervously.

"She laughed," the man persisted. "I heard her laugh and say, 'Shall I indeed bear a child, now that I am old?'"

Sarah came to the door of the tent and faced the man. "I did not laugh," she said anxiously. "But as you can see, I am not the age of women who bear children."

"Nothing is impossible for God," he replied.

"That is true," she agreed, and turned back into the tent. Abraham bade the men on their way.

The next spring, just as the stranger had promised, Sarah bore a son.

They called his name Isaac "because God has made laughter for me," Sarah said, her face full of joy. "Who would have believed that I would nurse a child in my old age?" Sarah smoothed the soft hair on the infant's head and thought of the Lord's promise. "Our descendants will be more numerous than the hairs on Isaac's head," she thought. "God will make of us a great nation."

The child Isaac grew. When he was three years old, he was weaned, and Abraham held a great feast in celebration. Isaac spent his days running after the young animals in the herd and playing with his older brother Ishmael. One day Ishmael was shooting arrows into the air, aiming at birds flying overhead. Sarah ran outside her tent where the boys were playing. "Do not shoot arrows near Isaac, you foolish boy," she shouted.

Ishmael aimed the empty bow at his younger brother. "Surely he can run faster than an arrow!" He laughed at Isaac, who ran to Sarah and hid.

That night, when everyone else was asleep, Sarah spoke to her husband. "Abraham, now we have a son. Just as God promised. Our own son shall be our heir."

Abraham took Sarah's hand. "God said I shall be the father of a multitude of nations. You shall be a mother of nations; God has said that kings of peoples shall descend from you."

"And what shall become of the child Ishmael? And his mother? It is not right that they remain here. All the lands as far as the eye can see will belong to my son and his descendants."

"But where would they go?" Abraham wondered. He fell asleep without an answer to his question. That night God appeared to him in a dream and told him that Sarah was right. Isaac was the child who would inherit Abraham's wealth. God would establish an everlasting covenant with Isaac and his descendants. But Ishmael would also be the father of nations because he was Abraham's son.

Abraham rose early in the morning and took bread and a skin of water and gave it to Hagar. Then he sent her away with her child to wander in the wilderness of Beer-sheba.

Sarah watched over her son and took great delight in him. She sat in front of her tent and imagined what his life would be like. God had indeed kept the promise. Their small pouches of silver had become sacks of gold. Their few flocks and herds had grown tenfold. And their son Isaac would be the father of a great nation. Surely God would want him to marry a woman from their own people, not one of the neighboring Canaanites. Was there a suitable girl in Haran, perhaps one of the daughters of her sister-in-law Milcah? Sarah lifted up her face into the warm sunlight and praised God. She had lived long enough to see the promise become real. Through her and Abraham all the people of the earth would be blessed.

NOTES

The stories of the patriarchs and matriarchs in the book of Genesis revolve around the threefold promise God makes to Abraham, the ancestor of Israel. Abraham/Israel will become a great nation; Israel will be given the land of Canaan; and Israel will be the means by which all peoples will receive God's blessing. No sooner is the promise given than various obstacles are introduced that threaten its fulfillment. For example, if Sarah is barren, how can she and Abraham have many descendants? Moreover, the

Bible says that both Sarah and Abraham are too old to have children. There is also the threat that Lot, when offered the choice of what territory to settle in, might choose the land promised to Abraham; or that Ishmael, and not Isaac, might be Abraham's heir. All the obstacles are resolved, however, as the ancient listeners knew they would be, since they were the heirs to the promise.

Our story follows essentially the biblical story line in Genesis 12–21, but we have conflated a number of the individual anecdotes and expanded them with material from later commentaries such as *Bereshit Rabbah, Pirke de Rabbi Eliezer,* and Rashi. *Bereshit Rabbah* and Rashi tell the story of Abraham's trying to hide Sarah in a box when they journey to Egypt. Her beauty became legendary: In rabbinic tradition Sarah is considered to be one of four women of perfect beauty. The others (they vary according to the source) include Abigail, Rahab, Rachel, Esther, Vashti, Michal, and Jael. The tradition that Hagar was the daughter of the Egyptian pharaoh is found in a number of ancient sources.

Hagar, the Mother
of the Ishmaelites

*H*agar ran through the fields, her sandals barely touching the ground. She ran to the edge of the grove of terebinth trees, she ran past the spring where Abraham's herdsmen watered the flocks, she ran until she had no more breath. She collapsed on a pile of stones to think about where she and her unborn child could go. After a while, she looked down at her swollen belly and cried out in a plaintive voice:

> *"I am weary with my moaning;*
> *My eye wastes away because of grief,*
> *it grows weak because of all my foes."*

Sarah had threatened her with a shepherd's crook. From the time she had been told that Hagar was pregnant, that petted old cow had treated her more harshly than the fresh Hittite handmaids who served in Sarah and Abraham's household. All the world praised her mistress, but Hagar knew better.

"Sarah is not the same in secret as she is in the open. She acts as though she were a righteous woman, but she is not righteous. She was not privileged to conceive all these years, and I became pregnant immediately." Hagar splashed some water from a nearby stream on her dirt-streaked face. She got up and turned toward the south. "Perhaps I could walk back to Egypt. Perhaps I could go back to my father's house where I could live in comfort again, and my child would receive the honors of a pharaoh's grandson."

Imagining her father's strong voice resounding through the marble council room, Hagar began to run again. In a little while she came to a spring of water in the wilderness, a spring on the way to Shur. "I will stay here and rest," she said to herself. "It will be days before I reach the palace of my father, the pharaoh of Egypt."

Hagar sat quietly in the silence of the afternoon. She had encountered no shepherds or herdsmen since she had fled from her Israelite mistress. The Egyptian princess felt herself alone as the single wispy cloud that paled the radiant sky above her. Suddenly she heard a voice. "Hagar, servant of Sarah, where have you come from and where are you going?"

Hagar covered her face with her hands. "I am fleeing from Sarah. She has dealt too harshly with me."

Again the angel of the Lord spoke. "Return to your mistress." Hagar began to weep loudly. She tore up handfuls of tiny purple flowers growing in the shelter of the moist rocks and threw them into the spring. "I will not return to that horrid place."

"You must return this night," the angel said. "Listen to me! God shall greatly multiply your descendants, so that they will be too numerous to be counted. The child you carry will be a son. You will call his name Ishmael, because God has listened to your lament. Your son Ishmael will be a rebel among people; he will be in need of others, and people will also depend upon him. All his days he shall live among his kin, sometimes in trial and anger, sometimes in peace."

When she heard this, Hagar fell upon her face and prayed aloud to God. "You are the God who sees everything. Truly I have seen God after God saw me." With her head held high, feeling the child stirring within her, she turned her face toward the land of Canaan to return to Sarah. "Did I really see God? Can one remain alive after seeing God?" she wondered.

The last rays of daylight were melting into the twilight sky when Hagar finally reached Sarah's home. Her mistress was watering the young lambs.

"I will water the lambs," Hagar said, knowing that was what she must do. With a few graceful movements Hagar took the large clay pitcher from her mistress's hands and finished the evening's work. Then without speaking to anyone she went into her tent and drenched her bed with tears. Neither she nor her mistress Sarah spoke of the day Hagar had fled into the desert searching for freedom. Hagar returned to the house of Sarah and Abraham as their servant. Only the shadows on her face spoke of her sadness.

Hagar bore a son to Abraham, and Abraham named him Ishmael. Sarah cherished the child and raised him as her own. To Hagar she was much kinder now that the Egyptian had given birth to such a beautiful baby. She offered her lentils from her own cooking pot; she made toys of brightly colored cloth for the boy Ishmael. Hagar grew accustomed to thinking of the boy as the son of Abraham and Sarah, a child she was free to love, but one who would inherit the gold of his other mother Sarah and the flocks and herds that she herself had tended.

After Sarah gave birth to a baby boy, however, she thought it was wrong that her boy should be brought up with Ishmael, who was older and might hurt Isaac after their father was dead. She watched Ishmael closely, but she no longer welcomed him into her tent.

Hagar spent more time with Ishmael, walking in the hills. She looked with pride at her strong son but feared that her joy in him might turn to mourning. Was there room in Abraham's tent for two sons? As Ishmael grew older, he spent his days learning skills from the herdsmen and his father, and he slept in the tent with his mother Hagar. He loved his younger brother and did not notice his mother's face growing dark with worry.

Abraham decided to hold an enormous feast and celebration for his son Isaac when the boy was about three years old. For many days everyone was busy with the preparations. Abraham himself ran into the herd and selected three calves to be prepared for the guests. He invited guests from far and near; Sarah used the finest flour to knead cakes. During the feast Hagar stayed in her tent, listening to the singing with a heavy heart.

"Why is Father holding a great feast with many guests for Isaac? Why is there no feast for me?" Ishmael asked his mother as the celebration lasted into the night. "Why is everyone congratulating Abraham on the birth of a son, when he already has a son?"

"Better is a dry morsel with quiet than a house full of feasting with strife," answered Hagar.

Ishmael shook his head at his mother impatiently.

"That's silly. I am going to join the singing." And he ran from her, no longer interested in the answer to his question.

The following morning before the sun was high in the sky, Abraham appeared at Hagar's tent. "You must leave here. Go, you and your son Ishmael, take your possessions and leave this land and go to a land that God will show you."

Hagar looked at him in horror. "But there is nothing in the wilderness but rocks and thorns. There is no spring, no road, no fields."

Abraham handed her a skin of water and a sack of bread. "Take this on your journey, and your son, and go now. For God has said that Isaac, the son of Sarah, shall inherit all the land and the flocks and the silver and gold. You and your son must go from Canaan. But do not be afraid. Ishmael is my son. God will be with the boy and make him a great nation also."

Hagar could not bear to hear another word. She ran out of the tent, grabbed the hand of her son, and fled. She did not stop running until they were out of sight of the tents of Abraham and Sarah.

When night fell, she gave Ishmael some bread and water, and then sat beside him while he slept. She tried to be calm, but fear was flowing through her as she thought of the endless days ahead in the wilderness.

> *"Be gracious to me, O Lord!*
> *See what I suffer from those who hate me,*
> *O you who lift me up from the gates of death,*
> *That I may recount all your praises.*
> *I will rejoice in your deliverance.*
>
> *"I call upon you, for you will answer me, O God.*
> *Incline your ear to me, hear my words.*

> *Wondrously show your loyalty,*
> *Delivering with your right hand*
> *Those who seek refuge from their adversaries."*

On into the night she prayed and scanned the cloudy sky for a sign. But none came. Hagar and Ishmael walked for a few more days, eating as little bread as possible, to make it last. They saw no berries or plants along the way. Nothing to eat except the bread Abraham had given them and the water in the skin.

"How much longer can we survive in this land of death?" asked Ishmael wearily. "I am too tired to walk any farther," he told his mother. He fell to the ground, resting his head against her knees. She gave him the remaining drops of water and watched beside him as he tossed in a feverish sleep near a spiky senna bush.

> *"Turn to me and be gracious to me,*
> *for I am lonely and afflicted.*
> *Relieve the troubles of my heart,*
> *and deliver me from my distress.*
> *Look upon my affliction and my trouble,*
> *and take away all my sins.*

"O God, grant me that I will not see the death of the child. Let me die first." Hagar turned away from the sight of her son. God heard Hagar weeping and called to her, "Hagar, do not weep. Awaken Ishmael. He sleeps beside you. I shall make him a great nation. Open your eyes!"

Hagar did as God commanded and when she opened her eyes, she saw a deep spring of cool water gushing beside her. She filled the skin and gave it to her son to drink and washed his face and her own, marveling in the precious water that God had sent.

N O T E S

We tell this story as a companion piece to "Sarah and the Promise." It is part of the same biblical story in Genesis 12–21, but where "Sarah and the Promise" emphasized Sarah's point of view, here we try to capture Hagar's perspective. The biblical text portrays Hagar's distress sympathetically. The story appears in two different versions, Genesis 16 and 21; we have combined them into one tale. In the story of Hagar the Egyptian fleeing oppression at the hands of her Israelite mistress, we have a reversal of the exodus theme, where Israel is delivered from oppression in Egypt. An important theme of the story is that Isaac's inheritance rights be guaranteed. Ishmael, along with his mother Hagar, must be expelled from Abraham's household because the covenant promises God made to Abraham are to be passed on through Isaac's line. Later they will be passed on through Isaac's son Jacob to his twelve sons, who represent the twelve tribes of Israel.

But Ishmael will also be the father of a great nation. He is the tribal ancestor of the Arabs. Thus, although the Arabs and Jews are two separate peoples, both trace their ancestry to Abraham. The Bible also views the descendants of Ishmael as related to the Egyptians: Ishmael's Egyptian mother Hagar arranges for him to marry an Egyptian.

As in "Sarah and the Promise," we follow the ancient tradition that Hagar was the daughter of the pharaoh of Egypt. Hagar's prayers are taken from the book of Psalms. God's appearance to Hagar with an announcement that Ishmael will be the father of a great nation corresponds to the divine announcement to Abraham concerning the future of Isaac.

Rebekah and Her Favorite Son

*I*saac was old and his eyes had grown too dim to see. He called Esau, his older son, and said to him, "My son, I am very old, and I do not know how many more days I have left on earth. Take your quiver and your bow, and go out into the fields and hunt some game for my supper. Then prepare the meat for me with sauce and seasonings; you know the way I like it. Bring me a meal of tasty delicacies, and then, after I have been strengthened by this special meal, I will pass on to you the ancestral blessing."

"I will fix you the finest stew," declared Esau. For he knew that his father had inherited the lands and the promise of God to make them a great nation through his father

Abraham. And Esau, as the eldest son, was entitled to the blessing of his aged father.

"I will give you my most precious blessing before I die."

Rebekah overheard Isaac's words to Esau and she hurried to find her younger son Jacob, Esau's twin brother. He was sitting outside the tent, resting in the shade of a tamarind tree. "What is it, Mother?"

"Hurry, bring me two kids from the flock behind the house, and I shall prepare that special stew that is your father's favorite. You must serve it to him so that you will receive his blessing, the one he received from his father Abraham."

"Now? Why such haste?"

"Just now I overheard him tell Esau to shoot some game and bring him a platter of delicacies so that he might receive the ancestral blessing. You must hurry," Rebekah urged. "We must carry out my plan if you are to receive the blessing that God told me was to be yours." As she spoke, Rebekah felt a chill blow across her skin. She had never told Isaac of the divine oracle that foretold the younger son's triumph over the older one. All these years she had held the secret close to her breast like a sleeping infant.

"But if Father means to bless Esau, why should he give the blessing to me?" Jacob asked as he got to his feet and looked toward the goat pen.

"There was a time for silence and now there is a time for telling," Rebekah said, looking with pride at the son who had owned her heart from birth. "When you boys were still thumping in my womb, the Lord spoke to me:

" 'Two nations are inside your womb
And two separate nations shall come forth from you.
The one will be stronger than the other
And the older shall serve the younger.' "

Jacob looked at her with amazement. "The older shall serve the younger," he murmured to himself as he went off to choose two kids from the flock. Rebekah's heart melted within her as she watched her son hurrying off to his task. He had always known how to please her. He had the gentleness of the flocks he tended. But Esau, the son as dry as the wind and as cold as the rain, never seemed to hold his mother in his sights. From the time he had been a young boy, he looked past her to the wildness and excitement of the fields that lay beyond their tents. Isaac was drawn to the boy's roughness and wrestled with him as he might with a young animal. As a child Esau had refused to learn. As an adult he was deaf to Rebekah and Isaac's fervent pleas that he not marry a Canaanite woman and instead married two of them.

Rebekah salted the meat Jacob brought her and mixed it with herbs and seasonings. "I can make this meal taste like the rich game the old man loves." She smiled to herself as her fingers worked the seasonings through the animal flesh. She chopped up vegetables and put them in the pot, not wasting a moment. Jacob walked around outside the tent, waiting for her to tell him what to do. His mother hummed as she worked. She had waited many years for this day. She knew that Jacob was worthy of the good fortune Isaac was about to communicate to him. It was God's will that the younger rule the older, and it was God's blessing that Isaac would award to her beloved Jacob.

Esau moved stealthily in the field, waiting for a sudden movement in the brush. A skilled hunter, he had no equal with a bow. "Now finally I shall get what I deserve," he thought. A few years earlier his younger brother had lured Esau into trading his birthright for a potful of rich lentil stew.

"This time I shall make the stew and I shall get the blessing. This time I shall not be tricked by Jacob. He was clever that day, getting me to find his lost lambs, tricking me with the aroma of my favorite lentils. He knew that after a day in the hills with a pack empty of game I would have given him anything to fill my aching belly. When he asked for the trade, I thought, 'What good will my inheritance be to me if I die of hunger?' He swallowed my birthright that day as surely as I swallowed the pot of lentils he held out to me. But that was long, long ago. That day will be forgotten when I have my father's blessing this day."

He sighted down the arrow and drew back the bowstring. "I shall be the clever one today. Jacob will not snatch the blessing the way he snatched the birthright. The one who makes the stew shall receive the blessing." He ran forward to collect the fawn whose flight his unerring arrow had stopped.

When Rebekah had finished cooking, she called Jacob to her. "Your father's eyes are dim. Put on these garments that belong to your brother. They smell of the fields, and your father will recognize Esau's strong scent on you."

Jacob held out his arms to his mother. "But I have smooth skin, and Esau's arms are thick with hair. If my father touches my hand, he will know that I have tricked him. Instead of his blessing I will bring his curse upon my head."

"If that should happen, may the curse fall upon me. If worse comes to worst, I am prepared to stand before your father and tell him, 'Esau is unworthy, and Jacob is a good man.' Now put on Esau's best clothes, and I shall cover your hands and the back of your neck with the skins of the kids from the flock."

"You are clever, Mother," Jacob said, laughing in admiration. "I would never have thought of such a ruse. Hairy skins from the flock will make me goatish like my brother Esau. And his animal-stinking clothes will certainly fool my father."

Rebekah closed her eyes and ran her hands over Jacob's arms. "You do feel like your brother." She handed Jacob the steaming dish of meat and bread that she had prepared. "Now go receive the blessing that God promised me was to be yours."

Jacob entered the tent where his father lay dozing.

"Father," he said softly.

"Which of my sons are you?" asked Isaac, shaking himself out of sleep.

"I am Esau, your firstborn. I have done as you asked. Please sit up and eat this delicious game so that you will be strong enough to pass on to me the ancestral blessing."

Isaac sat up and reached for the steaming dish of food. "However did you prepare this meal so quickly?" Isaac chuckled. "I must have dozed off. It seems as though I asked you to hunt the game only a few moments ago."

"I have brought you the meal with great speed because God granted me good fortune this day."

Isaac found it unusual for Esau to give credit to the Lord. The old man squinted through his nearly sightless eyes. "Come closer so that I may touch you and see if you are truly my son Esau. For the voice sounds in my ears like the voice of Jacob."

Jacob broke out in a cold sweat. He touched the goat-skin that covered his hands to reassure himself. Then, moving up to his father's bed, he held out his hands close to his father's face. Isaac stroked the hairy hands. "The voice may be the voice of Jacob, but the hands are the hands I know to be Esau's. Come close and kiss me, my son," Isaac said. He smelled the strong scent of the goats and the fields in Esau's clothes. He drew a deep breath and said:

"May God give you dew from heaven and rich produce from the earth,

May you receive in each season new grain and
  wine in abundance.
Nations shall serve you and peoples shall
  bow down to you.
You shall be master over your brother
and his descendants shall bow down to you.
Cursed be those who curse you,
and blessed be those who bless you."

No sooner had Jacob left his father's tent than Esau returned from his hunt. He set to work preparing the feast for his father. He seasoned the meat, chopped the vegetables, and, in spite of his excitement, took great care to make sure that the viands were succulent. "This will surely be the best meal my father could imagine." He sampled the stew again and smiled proudly as he licked his lips.

He hurried to bring the tasty dishes to his father. "Let my father sit up and eat from his son's game, so that you can bless me with the blessing of your father Abraham!" Esau's voice was full of anticipation.

"Who are you?" Isaac's confusion took Esau by surprise.

"Why, I am your son, Esau, your firstborn."

Isaac began to tremble until his whole body shook. "Then who was it that hunted game and brought it to me? He fed me a rich stew just before you came in. And I ate it and blessed him! Now he holds the ancestral blessing."

When Esau heard these words, he let out an anguished, bitter cry. "Oh, Father," he sobbed. "Jacob has snatched the blessing from me. What will become of me? You must bless me, too."

"Your brother used deceit to get the blessing I meant for you."

"It's not for nothing that his name means 'supplanter.' First he stole my birthright, and now he has taken away my blessing." Esau wept loudly. "Isn't there some blessing you could still give to me?"

Isaac's eyes were also full of tears. "I gave him every good thing. I made him master over you and all his relations. With grain and wine I have sustained him. What is left for me with which to bless you, my son?"

"One little blessing"—Esau's voice was thick with emotion—"please, bless me too, Father!"

"Come closer, my son." Isaac sighed and spoke wearily, as if each word had to be coaxed out of his mouth:

"The richness of the earth and the dew of heaven—
what shall you know of these blessings?
You will live by your sword,
and you will serve your brother.
But when you show signs of restlessness,
You will break his yoke from your neck."

Esau left his father's tent crestfallen. "While my father still lives, I will hold my peace. But after he is dead and the period of mourning is over, I will kill my brother Jacob."

Esau's words were repeated to Rebekah. She wasted no time in summoning Jacob. "Your brother Esau is consoling himself by planning to kill you. I have a plan. You must do as I say. You must go far away to Haran, where my brother Laban lives. He and his wife Adinah have two daughters, Leah and Rachel. You can choose one of them as a wife. Stay with Laban until your brother's anger subsides. When Esau has forgotten what you have done to him, then I will send for you. And you and your wives and your offspring shall live here in Canaan with me."

"But must I go now? Could I not wait awhile?"

"Your father is old, and could die at any time. When

that happens, Esau will surely carry out his threat to kill you if you are within his sight."

"But what if Father objects?"

"I shall convince him that this is the right course, my son." She looked at her son fondly. "I could not bear to lose both your father and you at the same time. You must save yourself and come back to me when your brother's wild temper has been tamed."

Rebekah went immediately to speak to Isaac. "I am sick to death for fear that our son Jacob might do as Esau has done and marry one of the local women. If Jacob marries one of these Canaanite women, what good will life be to me? Please send him away to Haran, to my brother Laban, so that Jacob can take one of his daughters as a wife."

"You are right, Jacob must not marry a Canaanite woman. Esau's wives have been too bitter for us to swallow. We must not have the younger son follow the elder one in marriage. Just as my father Abraham sent to Haran so that I might get a wife from among our people, so it is right for Jacob to select a wife from among our kinspeople."

"I will always remember how you looked in the field at twilight that first time I caught sight of you," Rebekah said.

"And you were so young and beautiful, with hair wavy, black as a raven." Isaac smiled contentedly. "Your voice still has the same happy melody in my ears that it did so long ago."

"I have never been sorry that I left my father's house and came here to you, to Canaan. And now Jacob must find a wife from among my people."

"We shall do as you advise." Isaac caressed his wife's hand.

The next morning Isaac called Jacob to him. "You must

leave our land and go to Haran, to the family of Bethuel, your mother's father, and choose as your wife one of the daughters of Laban, your mother's brother. May the Lord bless you and make of you a great nation. May the Lord grant the blessing of Abraham to you and to your offspring, and may you possess the land that the Lord promised to my father Abraham and to his descendants."

"I will do as you say, Father. And I shall be a worthy son to you all the days of my life."

Then Isaac sent Jacob to Haran, to Laban the son of Bethuel the Aramean, the brother of Rebekah, the mother of Jacob and Esau. On the morning that he left, Rebekah placed her hands on the head of her favorite son and gave him her maternal blessing.

"May the Lord of the world love you
as the heart of your affectionate mother rejoices in you,
and may the Lord bless you and your descendants forever."

NOTES

We first meet Rebekah in Genesis 24, which tells the story of how she is brought from her home in upper Mesopotamia, from where Abraham had migrated to Canaan, to become the wife of Isaac. In this story she is both generous in extending hospitality to Abraham's servant and ready to accompany the servant to Canaan without delay in order to marry Isaac. She shows similar initiative in Genesis 27, the story we retell here. Rebekah is instrumental in achieving what was ordained by God—that Jacob would be the recipient of the blessing. She orchestrates the deception of Isaac—Jacob simply follows her instructions—and she arranges Jacob's flight from Esau's wrath. According to Genesis 25, Rebekah was told by God that her younger son would take precedence over the older. Her death is not recorded in the Bible, and after his departure for Mesopotamia, Jacob never sees his mother again.

More than a solitary individual, Jacob stands for Israel, and his adventures represent Israel's struggles to make a home for itself in the land of Canaan, the land promised by God to Abraham and his descendants. The promise was passed down from Abraham to his son Isaac. Of Isaac and Rebekah's two sons, Jacob (Israel), and not Esau (representing Edom, Israel's neighbor to the south), is destined to be the recipient of God's promises. Jacob's roguish character reveals Israel's honest assessment of itself as not entirely worthy of the promise and yet tenacious enough to struggle for it. Upon his return to Canaan after a long absence, Jacob hopes to achieve a peaceful reconciliation by offering Esau a "gift." The word he uses, *berakhah,* is the same word used of the "blessing." Thus he symbolically offers Esau what had been stolen from him.

Deception figures prominently in the stories about Jacob; he deceives and is deceived by others. When Jacob is an old man, he is tricked by his sons in a manner that recalls Jacob's deception of his father. Just as Jacob uses Esau's clothes to deceive his father, Jacob's sons take the robe of his favorite son Joseph, smear it with blood, and lead their father to believe that Joseph has been torn apart by wild animals, while in reality they have sold him into slavery (Genesis 37).

Leah and Rachel, Matriarchs
of the House of Israel

From the time they were little girls, Leah and Rachel did all their chores together. As soon as it was light in the morning, the two girls went to the well to draw water for their mother. When Rachel was very little, she used to struggle with the heavy pitcher, and by the time she got back to their home, she had spilled most of the contents. Leah would laugh at the frown on her sister's face. "Don't be unhappy, Rachel. Before you can count to ten I will go back to the well and draw a fresh pitcher for you."

"I am so clumsy. I will never be careful and good like you, Leah, never spilling a single drop," said Rachel.

"Of course you will," her sister assured her.

A year passed and a second, and Rachel's hand grew steadier. She could outrun her sister and began to shepherd one of her father's flocks of sheep. Leah grew restless out in the pasture all day. She preferred spinning yarn near the tent. Rachel loved to lie on her back in the field and watch the patterns of clouds in the sky, fluffy and white like the sheep on the hillsides. "Look at the wind tossing those clouds around!" she called to her sister. "Aren't we lucky to live in this beautiful place?"

"I hope we are always this happy," Leah answered. Her life might be very different when she was married. She wondered if her father had been serious when he suggested that he might arrange a marriage for her with her cousin Esau, the son of his sister Rebekah. She had heard that he was horrible and gruff, a hairy man who roamed the hills, wild as a beast.

Soon Rachel began taking the sheep to graze alone. Leah cooked the meals and tended to the chores around the house. "Before you can count to ten, I will be back with the sheep," Rachel said in the morning when she left her sister at the well.

"Don't spill a single sheep," Leah answered with a laugh.

Spring turned to summer and the young lambs began to run with the flock.

After a journey of many days, Jacob reached the land of the people of the East. Before him he saw a well in a field. Lying beside it in the heat of the day were three flocks of sheep. "I will ask the people of this place if they know my mother's brother Laban or any of his family," he thought.

As he drew nearer, Jacob saw that the well was covered with an enormous flat stone. A few young men and women, the shepherds of the flocks, were sitting idly by the well, laughing and telling stories. Jacob approached them boldly, interrupting their talk. "Good day to you, my friends. What is this place called?"

"Greetings to you, stranger," they replied. "The name of this place is Haran."

Jacob was elated by his good fortune. "Then you must know Laban, son of Bethuel, son of Nahor."

"Yes, we know him. His tents are nearby—"

"How is he? Can you tell me anything about him?" Jacob continued eagerly. "Does his family prosper?"

"He's quite well. In fact, here comes his daughter Rachel with the flock."

Jacob could see a slim, graceful figure in the distance. "But isn't it too early to round up the animals? The sun burns high in the sky. Why don't you water the flock and take them to pasture?"

A shepherd with narrow eyes and a scraggly beard lost patience with the stranger's questions. "The well belongs to several families," he snapped. "We must wait until everyone's flock is here, so that all get their fair share of water."

"When all the flocks have been gathered, several of us roll the rock away and then we water the sheep," another shepherd said, pointing to the heavy stone that covered the mouth of the well. "As you can see, the rock is too large for one of us to move without help."

While they were talking, Jacob kept his eyes on the figure of the young shepherd woman advancing toward them. As she approached the well, surrounded by ewes and their nuzzling lambs, Jacob looked at her with pleasure. Her long dark hair fell across her face. When she smiled back at him, her teeth sparkled in the brilliant sunlight. Jacob bent to the stone and all by himself slid it off the mouth of the well. Glancing up at the young woman from time to time, Jacob watered the flock of his uncle Laban. When the sheep and goats had drunk their fill and wandered to graze the nearby grass, he looked at the young woman and said softly, "You are Rachel." He repeated her name again. "Rachel."

With tears in his eyes Jacob kissed his cousin Rachel. "I am Jacob, son of your father's sister Rebekah," he said, his voice trembling.

"You are Jacob?" Rachel asked. When he nodded, she hurried away to tell her father the news. Within a few moments the herdsman Laban returned to the well to greet his nephew. He embraced Jacob and escorted him back to his house. Jacob told his kinsman all that had happened in Canaan. "My mother wishes me to stay here with you," he concluded. "For it is from our people that I must take a wife."

"Yes, you must stay with us for a while," said Laban, "for you are my flesh and blood." He eyed the folds in his nephew's robes wondering if there were bags of jewels hidden there, such as the ones Abraham had sent with his servant when he came to find a wife for Isaac.

Jacob seemed to read his uncle's mind. "I have nothing except my energy and my willingness to shepherd your flocks. I got my father's blessing, and my brother Esau's anger drove me from Canaan without any of the wealth that one day will be mine."

A month passed, and Jacob worked hard for his uncle Laban. In the twilight after the day's work was done, he walked with Rachel and her sister Leah. "She is older, but I am faster," called Rachel as she ran across the pastureland toward an outcropping of rocks ahead.

"I can barely see her," Leah said, laughing. "Against the darkening sky, she is like a willow bending in the breeze."

Jacob could not take his eyes off Rachel. "Yes, she is graceful and supple as a young sapling."

Leah looked away from her cousin to cover her disappointment. He had eyes only for her sister. Before she could think of a way to remind Jacob that she was graceful too, Rachel had rejoined them.

"Leah thought you were a tree against the sky," teased Jacob.

"Leah had better be careful or she'll be trying to herd rocks, thinking they are sheep. My poor sister is afraid that she might have to marry your older brother Esau and she has cried her eyes out for so long that her eyes have grown weak."

Leah covered her face in embarrassment. "You shouldn't tell such stories."

"It is true. It is time for both of us to enter the marriage tent." Rachel looked directly at Jacob. "Father says the older for the older and the younger for the younger."

"An excellent saying it is," replied Jacob. His heart beat wildly as he imagined taking Rachel as his bride.

Several days later Laban came to Jacob in the evening while he was sitting outside his tent. "Even though you are my nephew, you cannot continue to work for me without wages. You are an excellent shepherd, a credit to your mother Rebekah. Set your wages, and I shall pay them."

"Uncle, there is only one wage I seek. I will serve you seven years if you will agree to let me marry your younger daughter Rachel."

"I would rather give her to you in marriage than to any other man. Stay and work with me, and she shall be yours."

For seven years Jacob worked for his uncle Laban. The flocks and herds increased, and Laban became a wealthier herdsman because of his nephew Jacob. As in the days before they made their agreement, Jacob walked with Rachel and Leah in the evenings. As they talked, Jacob counted out the days like shekels until Rachel would walk beside him as his wife. Finally the wedding day arrived, and suddenly the time seemed to have passed like a flash of bright coins to the happy bridegroom.

True to his word, Laban set about preparing for the wedding feast. He gathered together all the men of Haran and the wedding began. In the evening when the guests were full of wine, the men led Jacob to the marriage tent. In the dark night he embraced his wife, joyous that they were finally as one.

The following morning as soon as it was light Jacob awoke to find Leah asleep next to him. "How can this be!" he cried. "I've been tricked! Rachel was to be my wife! Why did you pretend to be your sister Rachel?"

"You should know about deception," Leah replied. "Didn't you trick your father by pretending to be your brother Esau?" She struggled to hold back her tears. Her husband had no more interest in her than in the delicately embroidered dowry cloths that decorated the tent.

Jacob jumped up and ran from the tent. He found his uncle Laban sitting in front of his tent, eating leftovers from the wedding feast. "Laban, you have gone back on your word. What have you done to me? For seven years did I not serve you for your younger daughter Rachel?"

Laban smiled and offered some goat's cheese to Jacob. But the younger man continued to shout. "Why have you deceived me? Why have you given me Leah?"

"In our country it is the custom for the older to be given in marriage before the younger. I will still allow you to marry Rachel. But first you must complete the week of marriage celebration with Leah. Then you may marry Rachel." He paused for a moment. "And of course serve me another seven years in return."

"Yes, yes, anything so that I may have Rachel for my wife."

When Leah heard of the agreement, the slice of mango

she was eating turned sour in her mouth. "My dearest Jacob shall be all mine for only one week. These seven days shall have to last my whole lifetime." By the time he returned from bargaining with Laban, she had dried her tears and greeted him with a proud smile. "Welcome to the wedding tent, husband."

After Rachel and Jacob were married, everyone saw that Jacob loved Rachel more than Leah. When he came in from tending the flocks, it was to Rachel he ran with the news of the day. As the weeks wore on, Leah grew sad because Jacob did not love her. She grieved silently, for she saw how much happier Jacob was when he was with Rachel than when he was with her. While Leah's days were filled with shadows, Rachel's were filled with sunlight. Soon Leah realized that she was pregnant and she rejoiced. "Surely when I give Jacob his first child, he will love me," she confided to her servant Zilpah.

Leah gave birth to a son, Reuben, and then to another, Simeon. And still Jacob preferred Rachel. And then Leah bore Levi, and still Jacob did not love her.

Rachel watched her sister tend her children and the sight of their joy made her sad. "I will die if I do not have children," she thought. "It is not fair that my sister Leah has so many sons while I have none."

Leah bore another son, Judah. The envy grew hard inside Rachel like a rock. "My sister's children increase; the flocks in the fields increase. But still I have no children of my own." The longer she watched Leah's children running after the flocks in the fields, the more the ache increased inside her. So she devised a plan. She called her husband Jacob to her and said, "You must have a child with my maidservant Bilhah, so that I may have a child through her." Jacob agreed, and Rachel named her infant son Dan. She loved the boy and made him toys of bright cloth, but still she longed for a son of her own.

One day during the days of the wheat harvest as Rachel and Leah sat in the courtyard making soap, Reuben ran to his mother. "Look at these odd roots that I found in the field!" He held up a handful of mandrakes. He dumped the plants in Leah's lap and ran back to rejoin his brothers.

"Oh, please give the mandrakes to me, dear sister." Rachel eyed the plants with fascination. "It is said that mandrakes have magical properties for women who cannot bear children. Perhaps they will help me."

"What help do you need?" scoffed her sister. "Jacob loves you best."

"But I have no child of my own."

Leah smiled. "Here you are, little sister. Take the mandrakes, and may God bless you with a child of your own. Please, all I ask in return is that you allow me to spend more time with our husband."

That night it was Leah who ran to greet Jacob, and Leah who amused him after the evening meal. And soon she bore him a fifth son, Issachar. Then God remembered Rachel, and she conceived a child. There was great rejoicing when Rachel's son was born. Leah celebrated with her sister, and together the two women sang and danced in delight. Rachel called the boy Joseph and prayed that God would bless her with yet another son.

When the number of Jacob's children was twelve, he called his wives Leah and Rachel to him in the field, where he was tending his flock. "There is something of great importance that we must discuss. I have lived here among your father's people for many years. Our flocks and herds have increased"—he gestured to the many animals spread over the land—"and we have great wealth. God has blessed us with many children, eleven sons and one daughter. The time has come to return to Canaan, to the land of my people, to claim the inheritance that God has promised to me."

"Are you certain the time is now, Jacob?" asked Leah.

"God came to me in a dream and said, 'Go forth from this land and return to the land of your birth.' "

Rachel and Leah discussed the matter between themselves and then replied to their husband. "We think our father has tricked you and played you foul. Not only in the matter of the marriage contract so many years ago, but also in the matter of the sheep and goats he promised to pay you for your labor. We know how he hid in the hills some of the best animals from each flock that should have been yours. But thanks to God, your flocks and herds have prospered in spite of our father. All the property that God has taken away from our father belongs to us and to our children; now then, whatever God has said to you, we want you to do."

So Jacob set out, with his wives Leah and Rachel and all of his family, and with all his cattle and all the livestock he had acquired in Haran, to return to the land of Canaan.

NOTES

According to Ruth 4:11, Rachel and Leah "together built up the house of Israel." They and their servants Bilhah and Zilpah, who became Jacob's wives of secondary rank, are the mothers of twelve sons who became the ancestors of the twelve tribes of Israel. The biblical story we retell here, found in Genesis 29–31, recounts the birth of eleven of Jacob's sons, explaining each of their names by a wordplay in Hebrew. We have not included all the details in our story, for the puns are impossible to capture in English. While in Haran, Leah gives birth to one daughter, Dinah, but Dinah does not become the ancestor of an Israelite tribe. Rachel dies in giving birth to Jacob's twelfth son, Benjamin, soon after they reach the land of Canaan.

Whereas Jacob had earlier deceived his father Isaac and his older brother Esau, in Haran he is deceived by his uncle Laban. Laban's explanation, "It is not the custom in our country to give the younger before the firstborn," maintains the right of the firstborn over the younger, a right Jacob disregarded in tricking his brother out of his birthright and in getting the ancestral blessing from his father. Leah's response, "You should know about the art of deception, for did you not trick your father by pretending to be your brother Esau?" is found in midrashic sources. So, too, is the explanation that Leah's eyes were weak because she had cried so much over the fact that she was destined to marry Esau.

According to tradition, Leah, the unloved wife, and Jacob are buried together in the ancestral tomb at Machpelah, along with Abraham and Sarah, Isaac and Rebekah. Tradition has favored a location outside Bethlehem as the site of Rachel's tomb, although Genesis 35 and some other biblical texts indicate a location north of Jerusalem.

Miriam's Well

*G*od has told us to leave Sinai where we were camped and to begin our journey again. We have been camped in the wilderness of Sinai before the mountain of God for many months. I am eleven, and my name is Yairah. I can still remember when we left Egypt in haste, and my mother loves to tell the story of the night our great leader Moses delivered to the people the word of the Lord God.

> *"I will pass through the land of Egypt that night and I will smite all the firstborn in the land of Egypt, both human and beast; and on all the gods of Egypt I will execute judgment. I am the Lord. The blood upon the doorposts shall be a sign for you,*

upon the houses where you are; and when I see the blood I will
pass over you, and no plague shall fall upon you to destroy you
when I smite the land of Egypt."

All our people repeat these words to remind us that God
has delivered us from the Egyptians and will bring us
safely to the land of Canaan, a land flowing with milk and
honey. Here at Sinai, God's holy mountain, we have received the commandments of the Lord God, who speaks
through the prophets Moses, Miriam, and Aaron. But we
have not yet come to the Promised Land.

Once again we have packed before daybreak, and as soon
as Moses gives the signal, we will set out. The sky is already
pale with heat. My hair is damp on my neck. By the time
the sun has whitened the sky, even the touch of damp hair
will be welcome. The people worked quickly to get the heavi-
est hauling done before the highest heat gripped the day.

As a special reward for having cared for my younger sisters and brothers for an entire week, my mother allowed me
to help Miriam pack her household goods in the cart and
travel alongside her. Miriam is older than my mother, but
she treats me with great seriousness. My mother laughs at
all my questions and calls me "Yairah why." But Miriam
answers each of my questions as though it had been put to
her by one of the elders of the tribe.

Miriam has been especially honored by our God. Wherever we wander in this wilderness, there is water. Wherever
we camp, there is a well, or spring, of water to refresh us
and our animals. Some say the well is God's gift to Miriam
for her devotion to God and to the people of Israel. Other
people say that the well accompanies us on our journey because Miriam gained much merit with God when she sang
the people across the sea during our escape from Pharaoh's
wrath. No one can truly know the divine reason for Miriam's well, but one thing I do know. Miriam is strong and

she makes us feel brave, even when there is no hint on the horizon of the land God promised to us, even when a land flowing with milk and honey seems to be only promised words flowing from the lips of our leaders.

A few days ago an extraordinary thing happened. God had told Moses to collect seventy of the elders and bring them to the Tent of Meeting. While we were not certain what was to happen, a thread of excitement wound itself through the camp. "What does God want of the men?" I asked Miriam.

Miriam, never one to waste a moment, was weaving a headcloth at a low loom. Her fingers flew across the threads as quickly as her words flew into the air. "We do not know for certain what God wants until we hear the divine word. Recently Moses has been feeling the weight of leadership and has asked God to help him with the burden."

"But Moses has you and Aaron to help him guide us. Why does he need more leaders?"

"It is a worrisome thing to lead so many. And now that some people are not satisfied with our journey and have been speaking out against Moses—"

"That is another thing I do not understand. For weeks now I have heard people wishing we were back in Egypt. One of my aunts says we will wither into dust before we reach the Promised Land."

Miriam wound blue thread through the woof and laughed. "Yes, I have heard such grumbling. 'In Egypt we had cucumbers and melons and leeks and garlic! In Egypt we had meat—fish from the Nile whenever we wanted.' Imagine, Yairah! God has given us this miraculous manna, just enough for each person to eat each day, and not a bit wasted. Still our people complain. Some people enjoy complaining more than the gifts of life."

I could not admit to Miriam that I was tired of manna instead of meals. When I thought "melon," my mouth ran with water of longing. "It makes me angry too," I replied, licking my tasteless teeth.

Miriam smiled at me with approval. "If it makes you angry, imagine how angry it makes our God."

"It is a good thing that God will send more help for Moses and you and Aaron." If only God would send some melons and garlic too. The manna that filled the stomach did not taste sweet or salty or pungent. Even bitter would be better than no taste at all.

At that moment Moses arrived at Miriam's tent. He looked directly at his sister Miriam but seemed not to notice me. "If all the fish in the sea were collected and piled up in our path, would that satisfy this quarrelsome people?"

"Sit for a moment, Moses. Yairah will get you cool water from the spring."

I hurried away and brought Moses a jug with water. He drank his fill and poured the rest over his head. Then he continued speaking rapidly. "Meat. The people want meat. And what am I to do? How can I be a mother to this people, Miriam? How can I carry this people in my arms, like a mother cradles her unweaned child?"

"Moses, you do not carry this burden alone," Miriam responded calmly. I have never seen her upset or angry. As she spoke, softly as my mother speaks to us when we are upset, Miriam continued to weave the cloth. A border of leaves was beginning to emerge.

Moses ran his fingers through his grizzled beard. "God has promised to send meat, God has said the people shall have meat for a month, but where will I find these mounds of meat? All the herds and flocks of all the people in the camp would not feed this people for more than a week. Miriam, why do the people crave meat?"

"You sound like little 'Yairah why,'" Miriam said, laughing.

Moses smiled at me and hurried off. Would there really

be meat? Would God ever provide us roast lamb again?

Later as the sun was setting, Miriam and I went to join the people outside the Tent of Meeting. No one was speaking. As God had directed, Moses had collected seventy of the elders and stationed them around the Tent. We continued to wait in startled silence. Even I could think of no questions to ask Miriam.

Suddenly the Lord God descended in a pillar of cloud. God spoke to Moses and whisked some of the spirit that was upon him and wrapped it upon the seventy elders. The wind blew and cries went up from the seventy elders. Now with this spirit, they too could hear the voice of God and prophesy to us the will of our God. I hid my face in Miriam's robe. Even buried in the darkness of the cloth, I squeezed my eyes shut so that I could no longer see. The thought of observing such a wondrous thing, to be standing in the presence of the Lord's spirit, overwhelmed me. My heart beat faster. Miriam seemed to understand my fear, for she held me tightly all the while the presence of the Lord was among us.

The men continued to prophesy until the sun died down in the west. The people were awed by what they had seen. "Will they continue to prophesy tonight, Miriam?" I whispered. The elders stayed in a group, amazed by what had happened, and did not move to rejoin their families.

"I think they will be silent again. The power of prophecy came upon them for a little while, for as long as it was the will of God that they prophesy."

When we returned to the camp, I paused to say good night to Miriam before returning to my mother.

A shout came out of the darkness. "The Lord will lead us to the Promised Land and that is the reason we have left Egypt. We shall wander through the wilderness. . . ." A crowd quickly gathered around the two young men, Eldad and Medad. "The spirit has come upon them," Miriam whispered to me. "Do not be afraid."

Although we could hear their voices, the murmuring of the crowd blurred the words of the two men.

Joshua, son of Nun, who had served Moses ever since we left Egypt came up to us. "Moses must stop them," he said, his voice rising with excitement. "They are prophesying."

"Moses cannot bear this burden alone," Miriam told Joshua.

But he shook his head impatiently. "I must find Moses. No one must recite the word of the Lord—"

"Why must you find Moses?" The voice of our leader Moses sounded weary. "Whatever has happened now?"

"Eldad and Medad are prophesying in the camp. Moses, you must stop them."

Moses laughed and turned to Miriam. "Imagine. Joshua is jealous on my account. What a foolish young man! If only all God's people could be prophets, if only all God's people had the divine spirit!"

Miriam walked off into the darkness with her brother, talking quietly about the wonders the Lord had performed for our people that day.

Throughout the night strong winds blew, so strong I thought our tent would be torn up from its pegs and tossed about over the rocky desert. But I hid my fear so that I could help my parents comfort my sisters and brothers. As soon as it was light the next morning, we heard people shouting from all sides. Flocks of quail surrounded the camp. Before my mother had braided my hair, I rushed out of our tent. All the people were gathering quail. In baskets and sacks. Piling the birds in stacks in front of their tents. They gathered them all day and all night and all the next day.

"At last we have meat to eat!" they cried. Some people

gathered more than they needed. "We shall eat so much meat that we shall never forget the taste of it again," they mumbled, the unchewed flesh still between their teeth.

My father forbade my brothers to capture quail. "But all the people are filling their bellies," objected Samuel. "Everyone is saying that we shall never be hungry again."

"Have you ever been hungry before?" My mother laughed at him until she discovered two quail he and Simeon had hidden under a sack of clothing. "No more of this sly business," my mother warned, shaking her finger at my brothers.

"Look, Daddy, I caught these all by myself. The small birds are everywhere. All over the ground. I can catch more." Little Sarah is my father's favorite, but he spoke sharply even to her.

"Put down those birds. You will not eat more than your fill," he insisted.

All around us people gorged themselves with quail until it came out of their nostrils. My mother hurried us inside our tent and kept us inside all that afternoon and evening. When we broke camp the next day, I saw mounds of earth piled up. My mother hurried all the children into the back of the cart. Many of the people had become sick from the quail and died within hours. My mother did not want us to see grieving families standing in tight groups, like flocks of birds, waiting for the men to dig graves.

The people were very frightened. The smell of death had replaced the odor of steaming meat. Without a word, as if they had been summoned by divine command, although God had not spoken, the people gathered outside the Tent of Meeting and called for Moses.

Finally Moses arrived, accompanied by Aaron and Miriam. "Surely you are not surprised at the stench of death in the air?" Moses asked, his voice low and harsh. The people pressed forward to hear his words.

"You recognize the smell of greed. It stings your nostrils the way anger burns in the nostrils of the Lord God. Death came to us because you are a greedy, foolish people. You did not trust in our God to provide food for each day," Moses said, raising his arms over his head. "We must leave this place, where our greed now rests in the ground."

Without being reminded, I did all my chores in preparation for leaving. I stayed close to my mother as we traveled to Hazeroth, where we pitched camp. For a couple of days there was a hush over the camp. People spoke very little to their neighbors. No one mentioned the quails. I did wish for melons.

But people forget the bad in life as well as the good. Things settled down, and I was comforted to see women spinning thread and weaving cloth outside their tents. Children began to play their old games when they watered the flocks. As I walked home from the spring, carrying a heavy pitcher of water, I thought of Miriam's story about the well. "God created the well of water just for us, God's special people, on the second day of creation." She is too humble to claim the divine gift of the well as her own. I think of her courage in singing our people across the Red Sea as they fled from Pharaoh's pursuing horsemen. I sing Miriam's song and I feel brave too.

*"Sing to the Lord, who has triumphed gloriously,
horse and rider God has cast into the sea."*

With the pitcher suddenly lighter, I ran all the way home.

As we attended to our chores during the day and sat by the campfires during the starry nights, the people began to complain once again.

"Moses spends no time with us anymore."

"Moses does not listen to our grievances."

"Moses inquires of the Lord almost every day. But what does he tell us of what God has revealed?"

Miriam had woven a new cloth for the priests to adorn the Tent of Meeting. I went with her to give the cloth to the priest who sat guard outside the tent where the libation bowls and incense burners were kept. For many days Miriam had been busy comforting the families of the dead and had no time for me. "It is not easy to explain the ways of God to people," she said. I did not reply for I saw that her eyes were darkly rimmed. She spoke to me with great effort as though she had been up for days nursing a sick child.

The voices of the people swirled like gnats around us as Miriam and I walked toward the Tent of Meeting. "Why do the people disobey God?" I asked as we presented the priests with the newly woven cloths.

"You don't ask easy questions, Yairah why," Miriam smiled, but her shoulders drooped. Her voice had lost its usual snap. "You anger your parents sometimes, don't you?"

"Yes, I act before I think," I admitted.

"That is precisely what the people do. I couldn't have described it better. And God is our parent, so God gets angry. Although it is not so easy to know why. For God does not always explain divine actions to us."

"Not even to you and Moses?"

Miriam shook her head. "No, my little one, for we are God's children too." She touched my cheek for a moment and hurried inside.

I did not see Miriam the following day for my mother had a list of chores for me to do as long as my braid. As I carried water and ground wheat for her, I thought what a heavy responsibility it must be for Miriam and her brothers to discern the divine will, to guide us so that we do not provoke the Lord God. For I have seen God's anger and I do not want ever to be in its path.

A few weeks later the grumbling had become louder and more frequent. The people did not still their complaints when Miriam or Moses or Aaron walked by. "Moses this, Moses that"—no wonder Moses looked discouraged. I knew that many people were complaining to Miriam and Aaron. I watched them lining up outside their tents. They went in looking angry and sullen and came out with the same frowns upon their faces. I was sitting a short distance from Miriam's tent when Aaron came to get her and together they walked over to the Tent of Meeting where Moses was.

"Moses, you cannot bear the sole responsibility for all these people," Aaron complained loudly. "You have taken it upon yourself to handle every problem as though it has befallen you. People feel cheated because you give more time to others than to them." At the sound of Aaron's angry voice, elders began to gather around the Tent.

"You should share this burden with Aaron and me." Miriam spoke more harshly than I had ever heard her! "You know that the Lord has spoken through us too. Why do you act as if you alone can discern the Lord's will?"

She turned to those of us standing near her. "Do you think Moses is the only person through whom the Lord speaks? Aaron and I are also the Lord's prophets. From now on, whenever you seek God's will, you do not need to inquire only of Moses. You may consult with Aaron or me."

Suddenly the pillar of cloud appeared at the entrance of the Tent of Meeting. The tension in the air was shattered by the voice of God: "How dare you criticize my servant Moses! To the prophets among you I reveal myself in visions or dreams, but to my servant Moses I speak face-to-face, plainly and not in riddles. How dare you make yourselves Moses' equals!"

As suddenly as it appeared, the cloud was gone. I gasped at the sight that met my eyes. Miriam's skin had turned white as snow! The people were terrified. "Look at Miriam's skin," someone called out. "She has been stricken with a foul disease!"

When I looked at Aaron, I began to weep. The anger of the Lord God had not touched him. Only Miriam bore the wrath of God. "It's not fair," I sobbed through my tears. "Won't someone help her?" I began to run to Miriam, but people held me back. "You cannot touch her. She has been struck by God."

Aaron stepped forward and clutched Moses' robe. "Oh, dear brother, do not let our beloved Miriam be punished for the sin we have been foolish enough to commit. Please do not let her become like one dead whose flesh is half eaten away in the grave."

Miriam sat like one in sleep. Her face held no trace of fear; she did not cry out, nor did she examine her blistered skin. She sat on the ground, her horrible white hands lifeless in her lap. The people had moved away from her, leaving a circle of emptiness surrounding her.

Moses embraced his brother and then took a few steps forward. "O Lord God of Israel, who has carried us like a mother carries her child, I beg of you, I plead with you, please heal our dear Miriam."

In a moment God spoke to Moses. "Suppose her father had punished her by shutting her in their tent. Would she not have to remain there for seven days? So then I shall have her shut outside the camp for seven days. After that time, she may be brought in again."

Miriam got to her feet and walked to the outskirts of the camp. Moses and Aaron walked with her to the southern border. My mother restrained me. "You must not follow her."

"Can I bring her water from the spring?"

"You must ask Moses before you approach Miriam," my mother said. But while she spoke, she studied my face.

"You are not afraid of the disease that has struck Miriam, little one?"

"Of course not," I replied angrily. "Miriam is good and she obeys the word of God. She will be leading our people again. I know that as surely as I know that you will tell me it is time to do my chores."

My mother hugged me. "I am proud of you. Now, go, fetch fresh water from Miriam's well. And leave the pitcher at the southern border of the camp."

For seven days I left water morning and evening for Miriam. As I drew the water from the spring, I prayed that God would remember the merit of Miriam that had brought us bountiful water all these years.

For seven days the people spoke in praise of Miriam. Her trouble made them realize how much they depended on her. "We shall not break camp until Miriam has been healed," the elders declared.

At sunset on the seventh day the people gathered at the Tent of Meeting, and we all walked with Moses and Aaron to the southern end of the camp. It was a joy to behold Miriam, healed and smiling, waiting to be received back into the camp.

"The Lord is my strength and my song," sang Miriam. "The Lord has become my salvation. For God has led in steadfast love the people whom divine care has redeemed."

The people lifted their voice in response to Miriam's song.

> *"Who is like you among the gods, O Lord?*
> *Who is like you, glorious in holiness,*
> *inspiring praises, working wonders?"*

I ran to embrace my dear friend Miriam. Her skin had its healthy glow. There was no trace of the disease upon her.

That night Miriam led the women in singing and dancing, with timbrels and tambourines. The following day we broke camp and continued our journey, with Miriam and her brother Moses leading us on our way. Miriam's well accompanied us as it always had.

Several years later, shortly after my first child was born, Miriam died and was gathered to her people. After that sad time, our well dried up and we experienced a terrible drought. People say the well went dry because God had given us the well only while Miriam lived, a prophet for her people.

NOTES

The biblical tradition has not preserved much information about Moses' and Aaron's sister Miriam. The second chapter of the book of Exodus tells how Moses' mother saved the life of her infant son by setting him afloat in a basket on the Nile. Moses' older sister watched over him, and when the basket was discovered by the pharaoh's daughter, she brought her mother to be the boy's nurse. In this story the sister's name is not given. That Miriam was recognized as a leader of the people is clear from her victory song at the crossing of the sea in Exodus 15:20–21, and from Micah 6:4, which names her along with Moses and Aaron as leaders of the exodus.

The story we tell here is based largely on the book of Numbers, especially chapters 11 and 12, and deals with the journey of the Israelites to the Promised Land after their deliverance from bondage in Egypt. In the account of Israel's journey from Egypt to Sinai to the Promised Land, preserved mainly in the books of

Exodus and Numbers, two themes are prominent: the negative theme of the people's continual complaining, and the positive theme of God's providing for the people's needs, leading them on their journey, and sustaining them with food and water. The book of Deuteronomy adds that during the forty years the Israelites spent in the desert their clothes did not wear out and their feet were not swollen.

The basis of Miriam and Aaron's complaint against Moses is not clear. The biblical text says that they criticized Moses because of the Cushite woman he married, yet the substance of their complaint indicates that the issue is leadership, specifically Miriam and Aaron's claim to equal authority with Moses.

Miriam's death is reported in Numbers 20. It is followed by a story about the people's complaining because they have no water. Rabbinic tradition fills the gap between the two stories with a midrash that attributes the gift of water to Miriam's righteousness: Miriam's well follows the people throughout their journey; when she dies it dries up.

Eluma and Hannah

*E*luma was sitting in the field in the shade of a tamarisk tree. She had been planting wheat since the early morning, and now that the sun was high in the sky and it was too hot to work, she was taking her midday rest. Her husband Manoah and some of the other men were pasturing goats near the Danite settlement. "Arguing and planning, planning and arguing, what they can do to thwart the Philistines. Greedy Philistines, who swallow our parcels of land like so many morsels of bread. Our most fertile fields in the north now raise Philistine crops. And now they have their eyes on the land to the south," she thought. As she looked at the rich soil that stretched out before her, waiting to receive the summer crop, Eluma wondered if the tangle of Israelites and Philistines would ever work itself out. "There isn't enough land for all of us, Israelite and Philistine, to grow crops and pasture flocks and herds," she muttered as she lifted her water jug to her mouth. "When will God do something to ease our suffering?"

Without warning, a shadow fell across the ground before her. Eluma was startled to see a stranger in the field. From his appearance, she saw that the man was not a Philistine.

Before she could open her mouth or get to her feet, the stranger began to speak. "Eluma, wife of Manoah, of the tribe of Dan, you have not petitioned the Lord God pleading for a child, but now you will conceive and bear a son. He will be the first to deliver Israel from the hands of the Philistines. You shall drink neither wine nor beer nor eat anything unclean, for the boy will be a Nazirite dedicated to God. No razor shall touch his head, for if his hair is cut, God's power will leave him."

The woman looked at the stranger in amazement. Could God indeed be acting to bring peace from the threat of the Philistines? It was true that she and Manoah had no children. They had wanted a child, but when it became clear that Eluma could not conceive, she had shut her dreams out of her mind. No use wishing for what is not to be. "This man must be a prophet of God," she thought, "to bring such news." Without a word to the stranger she ran from the field to tell her husband what had happened.

She caught sight of Manoah near the spring, watering the goats. "Manoah!" she cried out, waving her arms wildly.

"Catch your breath," he replied, putting his hand on his wife's shoulder. "Here, drink some water."

Eluma gulped a few swallows of water and continued rapidly, "A miraculous thing has happened! A man of God appeared to me! A prophet! He looked like an angel of God. He appeared suddenly to me in the field. I do not know where he came from, and I did not ask his name."

"A prophet? What did he say?" Manoah asked.

"He told me that we shall have a son. He said that I must drink no strong drink and eat nothing unclean. For the boy will be dedicated to God as a Nazirite even before he is born. And he will remain a Nazirite until the day of his death."

"That is wonderful news indeed." Manoah embraced his wife.

That night, as Manoah tossed about in bed, he began to wonder why the man of God had appeared to his wife and not to him. "I beg you, O Lord God," he prayed, "let the prophet you sent appear again, this time where I am tending the flocks. Let him come again and instruct us about the boy whom Eluma is to bear." Manoah finally fell asleep, certain that God would come to him since God had already so honored his wife.

The next morning he left his wife earlier than was his habit and drove the goats to pasture. He barely gave a thought to the animals, for his eyes stayed upon the horizon, waiting for the stranger to bring news of his son. "If God has heard my prayer, God will send the prophet to me this day," he assured himself. Once he thought he saw a sign of a man approaching, but it was only the shadow of a goat that had strayed to the edge of the pasture. "Can it be true," he wondered, "that God intends to bless us with a son? Perhaps Eluma was planting too long in the sun yesterday."

Eluma was once again sitting in the field taking her noonday rest. A son to help with the flocks and herds. A son who would save all Israel! "Such nonsense," she thought. "Dreams are for those who do not have seeds to plant." All of a sudden he was beside her, the man whose specialness caused ripples along her flesh.

Once again, saying not a word to the stranger, Eluma

bolted to her feet and ran to get her husband. "Manoah," she yelled as loud as she could, "come quickly. The prophet is in the field."

Manoah ran after his wife. The prophet was still standing by the tamarisk tree. Indeed, he was no Philistine. His clothes were unlike those of Manoah. "He does not look like a herdsman," Manoah thought. Eluma reached the man first and urged her husband to hasten. "Are you the man," he panted, "are you the one who spoke to my wife yesterday?"

"I am."

"Then tell me what I want to know. When your words come true—your words about the son who will be born to us—what is to be the boy's manner of life? What will become of him?"

"I have already told your wife," the stranger replied. "She must follow my instructions. She must drink neither wine nor beer nor eat anything unclean." His face contained no expression as he spoke. His eyes did not look directly at either husband or wife, but rather he stared above their heads, as though words were written there.

Manoah looked quizzically at the man of God, waiting for him to say more. But the man was silent. Perhaps if he could speak with the man without Eluma standing by so eagerly, as if she had discovered the man, when it was the man who had come upon her.

Finally Manoah said, "May we offer you our hospitality? Surely you must be hungry coming from such a distance. Let us prepare a meal in your honor."

The messenger of God replied, "I will not eat food. But if you wish, you may prepare a sacrifice and offer it to God."

While Eluma was preparing for the sacrifice, Manoah tried to engage the man of God in conversation. "Tell me your name, for we would like to honor you when your words come to pass."

"Why do you ask my name? Like my message, it is wondrous."

"But to honor you, when the boy comes," Manoah persisted.

Eluma returned to them and thrust into her husband's arms the young goat to be sacrificed. "Perhaps," she said, "the prophet wishes to rest while we finish preparations for the sacrifice." From the beginning she had felt the specialness of this reserved man. His words were carefully measured, like the grain for the offering. She wished her husband wouldn't throw so many words into the man's path. Hadn't the messenger already told them what they needed to know?

Manoah took the young goat and the cereal offering and, using a rock as an altar, offered them to the Lord.

Then, while Eluma and her husband watched, the Lord worked a wonder. As the flame from the altar flew heavenward, the messenger of the Lord ascended in the flame in full view of Eluma and Manoah. Stunned by what they had witnessed, they fell upon their faces on the ground. When they arose awhile later, the messenger of God was nowhere to be seen. The air was still and clear and no one was in the field.

"We have seen an angel of God." Manoah's voice quavered. "We shall surely die, for who can see such a wonder of God and live!"

Eluma, who understood that what she sensed about the man of God was true, reassured her husband. "If the Lord had meant to kill us, the Lord would not have accepted this offering from our hands or allowed us to see this wonder. Surely God does not desire our deaths, for God has told us that we shall have a son who will begin Israel's deliverance from the Philistines."

Manoah nodded his agreement. God had chosen them to

be the parents of a child who would grow up to defeat the Philistines.

When the child was born, Eluma named him Samson. "He is a ray of sun in my life," she laughed. "His name will be famous among our people for all time."

In the hill country of Ephraim lived a man named Elkanah, who had two wives. One was named Peninnah and the other was named Hannah. Peninnah had many children, but Hannah had none. While they baked bread and trimmed the lamps, Peninnah's mocking laughter followed Hannah. "You can gather the herbs from the hillsides and the fruits from the trees because I have children to care for."

"Elkanah loves me best," Hannah thought to comfort herself, but she never spoke these words to Peninnah. Rather she would hum a tune until the other woman got tired of taunting her. But it seemed as if Elkanah's other wife would never stop teasing Hannah. "Have you fed your children this lovely morning?" she would ask as Hannah went by to draw water from the well. After years of taunts, it was no longer possible for Hannah to cover her pain. Lines of sadness enclosed her eyes.

Once a year Elkanah and his family went up to Shiloh to offer a sacrifice to the Lord God. Dressed in their finest clothes, their cart piled high with a generous offering for the Lord, they set out on pilgrimage, their piety an example to the other families of Ramah. As they approached the great stone altar, they saw Eli splendid in his long blue linen robe, woven with threads of pure gold and silver. On special festival days he wore the fine garments that could be worn only by the high priest when he was performing the holy rites on behalf of the people of Israel. His sons Hofni and Phinehas stood on either side of him. The air was redolent with the odor of the burnt offering. An odor that would surely please the Lord God and bring continued divine bounty to the people of Israel.

"In thanksgiving for all that God has given us during this year, for the crops which have burst forth from the fields and for the herds which have multiplied," said Elkanah as he presented the offering to the priest.

Year after year, Elkanah, Hannah, Peninnah, and Peninnah's sons and daughters went to make the special annual sacrifice. Hannah felt as though she had made the long trek from Ramah alone. When they shared the sacrificial meal, Elkanah always awarded his beloved Hannah a portion as large as Peninnah's. But in Hannah's eyes, what she received seemed small compared with the bounty of Peninnah's portion. The other woman had daughters, the other woman had sons. As the three of them retreated from the Holy Place, Hannah wept.

"Why do you weep? And why have you not eaten during this journey?" Elkanah asked her. Hair strayed from under her headscarf, like kids from the herd. When he had married her, Hannah would never have allowed wisps of hair to fly around her face.

Hannah looked at him and said nothing. He asked about her tears when they went up to Shiloh each year and when they returned from the pilgrimage, but he knew well why she cried. For God had chosen to close her womb and make her unlike other women.

Elkanah looked at his wife with sadness. "Do not weep. Am I not more to you than ten sons?"

"Yes, you are a good husband," she said sadly. But the salt of her tears remained bitter in her mouth. She sat for a time with Elkanah and Peninnah. Then she rose and went by herself to pray before the ark of the Lord. She was so wrapped in thought that she did not notice Eli the priest sitting at the doorpost of the temple. She vowed a vow deep in her heart and prayed, "O Lord of hosts, if you will look

on the affliction of your humble servant Hannah and remember me and bless me with a son, then I will give him to
your service as a Nazirite all the days of his life. He shall
drink no wine nor beer and eat no food that is unclean. No
razor shall touch his head."

While she prayed, her lips moved ever so slightly. She
rocked gently back and forth, lost in her vow to God, while
Eli watched from the doorway. When she did not arise
from her position, but continued to move her lips with no
words coming forth, Eli approached her. "How long will
you sit here, drunk, before the Lord? Put away your wine,
woman, and leave this place."

"Oh, good Eli, no drop of wine has touched my lips. I am
deeply afflicted and have been pouring out my soul to the
Lord God that my pain shall be lifted."

"Then go in peace. And may the gracious God of Israel
show you mercy and grant your petition."

So Hannah rejoined her husband and ate her fill, and
laughter returned to her mouth. Early the next morning
before they returned to Ramah, they went once again to
pray before the Lord. Hannah prayed with peace in her
heart and the Lord remembered her. Within a year she gave
birth to a son. "We shall call him Samuel because I asked
him from the Lord and the Lord answered my prayer."

When it was time to make the yearly pilgrimage to Shiloh, Hannah did not wish to go. She went to the cart where
her husband had placed the animals for the sacrifice. "I
shall stay at home with my small son. As soon as he is
weaned, I will bring him to the temple at Shiloh, so that he
may be dedicated to the service of God, and he will remain
there for all the days of his life."

Elkanah had never known such joy. For Hannah sang as
she went about her work and each day did not seem long
enough to hold all her laughter. The trouble between her
and Peninnah seemed to have been put to rest. Hannah's

son had brought peace to the family, like rainfall after a drought. "So whatever seems best to you, dear wife, that is what shall be done with the boy. Wait until you have weaned him, and then he shall be dedicated to God."

And it happened just as Hannah had vowed to God. When Samuel was three years old, Hannah took the boy to Shiloh along with an offering to give thanks to God: a three-year-old bull, half a bushel of flour, and a skin of wine. Full of pride, Hannah presented the boy to Eli the priest. "Remember, good Eli, I am the woman who prayed before the ark of the Lord and the Lord granted my petition. So I wish to lend to God this greatest joy of my life that he may bring joy to God, serving all the days of his life here with you at the temple of the Lord."

And Hannah and her husband Elkanah worshiped God and Hannah prayed.

"My heart exults in the Lord
  and my strength is exalted in the Lord.
  My eyes look past my enemies
  because I rejoice in God's salvation.
  There is none holy like the Lord God
  no one except you, O Lord.
  There is no rock strong like our God.

"So talk not in pride, O people of Israel,
  let not arrogance stream from your lips
  for the Lord is a God of knowledge
  and by the divine judge are all earthly actions weighed.

"The bows of the mighty have been broken
  and the feeble now gird on God's armor.
  Those whose bellies hung low with fat
  now hire themselves out to earn their bread.
  And those who ached with hunger now eat their fill at God's table.
  The Lord makes poor and rich; the Lord brings low and exalts."

The young Samuel remained at the temple at Shiloh wearing the linen ephod as a servant of the Lord. From time to time his mother would make him a little robe and bring it to him when she and Elkanah came to make their sacrifice to God. Eli the priest of Shiloh would welcome them at the gates of the temple, saying, "May God bless you with many children in return for the gift of this marvelous boy that Hannah has dedicated to God!"

And Hannah looked toward the temple of God full of happiness. "My heart exults in the Lord," she said and turned to smile at her husband.

NOTES

Our story juxtaposes two biblical birth accounts, Samson's (Judges 13) and Samuel's (1 Samuel 1 and 2). Both are stories of the birth of a son to a barren mother, a common biblical motif that allows God to intervene to bring about the birth of the hero (as in the stories of Sarah and Rachel). Both children are apparently consecrated from birth as Nazirites; following the Greek and the Samuel scroll from Qumran we have emphasized the Nazirite motif in the Samuel story. Nazirites were men or women who dedicated themselves to God for a specific period of time during which they could not drink strong drink, cut their hair, or come into contact with the dead; rules concerning the Nazirite are found in Numbers 6. Samson, and probably Samuel, are the only examples of lifelong Nazirites. In Samson's case, his mother must keep the Nazirite obligations during her pregnancy. In the Greek and Qumran versions, Hannah's vow also involves keeping these obligations.

There is no indication in the biblical story that Samson's mother longed for a child. Her husband does not pray for her to conceive, as Isaac prays for Rebekah; she does not complain to her husband about her childlessness, as Rachel complains to Jacob. Nor does she try extraordinary means of procuring a child, as Sarah and Rachel do.

The biblical storyteller describes Hannah's longing for a child, but Hannah does not scheme the way Sarah and Rachel do to get a child. She alone of all the barren women in the Bible simply asks God to give her a child. In addition to Samuel, Hannah and Elkanah later have three sons and two daughters.

The women's stories are recorded because of their famous sons. The Bible does not give the name of Samson's mother. We call her Eluma, following Pseudo-Philo; Midrash Rabbah to Numbers records her name as Hazlelponi. Though unnamed, Samson's mother figures prominently in the narrative. She has greater theological insight than her husband Manoah. She senses something special about the messenger's identity from the beginning, and when the messenger's identity is revealed, she recognizes the divine purpose behind the events. Manoah, for all his efforts, never receives as much information from the angel about the child as she does. Hannah's fervent prayer for a son and her willingness to give him to the Lord's service if God will grant her prayer emphasize her faithfulness, for which she is rewarded, and show her to be the ideal mother for the great prophet Samuel.

Naomi and Ruth

*O*nce upon a time, in the days when the judges judged, there was a great famine in the land of Israel. In Bethlehem of Judah a man named Elimelek let the parched stalks of grain fall from his soil-stained hands and knew he must leave his land. He took his wife Naomi and his sons Mahlon and Chilion and left the fields that he had tilled until the harvests had become too meager to feed them. Setting their faces toward the east, they left Bethlehem in search of bread.

After traveling for several days, they came to the land of Moab. They saw that grain grew in the fields and that the land was fertile. They decided to sojourn there. Soon after the first harvest, Elimelek died, and Naomi gathered her two sons close to her to comfort her. For in a strange land without any family, they were all she had.

When the time came for the sons of Naomi to marry, they selected Moabite wives. Chilion married Orpah and Mahlon married Ruth. They lived in the land of Moab with Naomi, their mother, for ten years. In the springtime, before the barley harvest, Chilion and Mahlon died. Naomi mourned her sons in a strange land. She was all alone.

A short time later Naomi called Orpah and Ruth to her. "Gather your few belongings. I have heard that the famine is over in the land of Israel and I want to return to my people. There is bread here in Moab, but I have a hunger for my homeland."

The very next morning as soon as the sun was seen in the sky, the three women left the house where they had lived for ten years, and with their few belongings and the memories of their husbands, they set out for Judah. When they crossed over into the valley where the family of Orpah lived, Naomi stopped. "It is time for us to part. Each of you must return to her mother's house. May the Lord be as kind to you as you have been to my poor dead sons and to me. I pray that the Lord will provide a splendid home for each of you, each in the house of a new husband." The old woman gently touched each young woman's cheek.

Orpah and Ruth embraced each other and clasped Naomi's hands. "We will not leave you to find your way through these lonely valleys alone to your homeland. We will go with you." They both wept, but Naomi turned away and examined the cloudless sky. "It is time for me to be on my way. Now go, each to her own home."

Naomi walked a few steps until her daughters-in-law blocked her path. "We will return with you."

Naomi lowered her sack of belongings to the ground. "Why should you follow me one more step? What have I to offer you? Will I ever bear sons who can be husbands for you?" She laughed sharply. "And if by some miracle God filled my shriveled womb with sons, would you wait, unmarried, growing older by the day, until they became of marriageable age? Would you sit alone until you were old and bitter as I am now to receive the protection of marriage? You must go home and you must find husbands." She looked away from their tear-soaked cheeks, for her eyes had cried their last tears in mourning for her sons.

Orpah reached into her small sack of clothes and handed Ruth a silver ring. "Take this ring, my sister, and remember that we will be sisters until the day of our death. No matter into whose house we go." Weeping and shaking with sadness, Orpah turned away from Naomi and Ruth and went down into the valley, to the house of her mother.

Naomi looked at the ring on Ruth's finger. "Now you too must go back to your people and to your gods, just as Orpah has done. I am old and bitterness is my companion, now until the day of my death."

But Ruth took her mother-in-law's hand and held it firmly. "Do not ask me to leave you. Do not demand that I turn away from you. For where you go, I will go, and where you live I will live. Your people shall be my people, and your God shall be my God. Where you die, I want to die, and there I want to be buried. May God strike me down if anything but death separates me from you."

Naomi saw the determination on Ruth's face. Saying nothing more, the old woman shouldered her burden and walked on.

They journeyed northward across the Arnon River and rested. Day after day they walked across the plains of Moab. They had to choose their route with care so that they could refill their skins with water from the wadis. The way was hard, and the women spoke little. They crossed the mountain passes and finally Naomi sat down to rest upon a barren hillside. A thin smile crossed her face. "It is the Jordan valley. The river flows below. We are near home."

As the two women came near Bethlehem, Ruth looked at the green fields and the plump olive trees and widespread almond trees silhouetted against the sky. "It is so beautiful, so green with life." In a few moments they were in the middle of a field of bright red flowers. Ruth bent to pick some for Naomi. "What are these flowers?" she asked as she handed the flowers to her mother-in-law.

"Anemones," said Naomi and let the flowers fall to the ground.

"The time of harvest brings such joy to the earth," said Ruth.

"We are near the town."

As they entered the town square, the women of the village gathered to meet them. "Is it Naomi?" they cried.

"It is Naomi." The women of Bethlehem pressed close to Naomi and Ruth. "Your hair was dark as the night when you went away. And now it has grown gray," one of the women exclaimed. "Sweet Naomi, we have missed you!"

"Do not call me sweet," she said.

"This is my child," a woman said, an infant in her outstretched arms. Naomi turned away as though the child were a demon. "Do not speak to me of children. For my sons lie in the earth in Moab alongside their father. I left Bethlehem full and I have returned empty and old, bitter and alone."

The women exchanged uncomfortable glances and picked up their water jugs. "We must get back to our homes. The workers will be returning from the fields," they said, not wanting to look at the hunched figure and the young woman who stayed silently by her side.

"Everyone is busy during the time of the barley harvest," Naomi said. "When the harvest is full and the fields are fat with grain, the village knows nothing of bitterness."

The next morning Ruth said to Naomi, "Please let me go to the fields. I can glean after the harvesters in the field of whatever landowner will permit me. Then we will have food to eat and you will truly feel as though our journey has ended."

"Go, my daughter, and I shall fill our vessels from the well."

So Ruth took her empty sack and gleaned in the fields that had already been harvested. Soon she came to a part of the field where the stalks stood tall and the young men and women were bent to their work. "This would be a good place for me to find much grain," Ruth thought.

"So you are the Moabite woman, the one who returned with Naomi last night?" the overseer asked her.

Ruth smiled. Word spread as quickly in Judah as in Moab. "Yes, we have come home," she answered simply. "Would the owner of this field allow me to glean for my mother-in-law, for Naomi? We have brought nothing with us, and we have no one to provide for us."

"Yes, my master is generous to those in need. For the orphan, the sojourner, and the widow, there is always something. You many glean after the harvesters." He looked at the young woman, whose hands were not marked from the work of the fields. "Be alert. The young men, sometimes, they are high-spirited." He turned away.

Ruth set to work and followed the workers, up one row of barley and down the next. Occasionally one of the young men would lag behind his companions and stare at her. But the work was hard, and they had no time for foolishness. Not during the height of the barley harvest.

From the corner of her eye, Ruth saw a tall man in a bright robe speaking to the overseer. As they talked, the overseer pointed toward her. Embarrassed, Ruth crouched lower, over the sheaves. It must be the owner, she thought, as the workers stopped in their work and bowed toward him as he inspected the work. He was walking toward her, she realized, and she reached up to smooth her hair.

"Hello, daughter—"

"I have permission, my lord, to glean in your part of the field. If it is well with you." She bowed.

"Of course, you must glean here and in the field of no other man in Bethlehem. Do not go to another field. But stay close to the young women. I have ordered the young men not to annoy you. And when you are thirsty, go to the water jugs and drink your fill. I, Boaz, have commanded it."

Overcome with his generosity, Ruth fell to the ground and bowed. "Why have I found favor in your eyes? I am a foreigner, a Moabite. Why should you take notice of me?"

Boaz put his hand on her shoulder. "All the kindness you have shown to your mother-in-law Naomi has been reported to me. I know that after the death of your husband, you left your land, and your father and your mother, to come to the land of Israel to live with a people you did not know before. May God reward you for what you have done, and may the Lord God of Israel spread a cloak of refuge for you. From this day forth you may seek protection here."

"You have been so kind to your humble maidservant, even though I am not even one of the workers of your field."

When it was time for the noonday meal, the harvesters hurried to the jugs of water mixed with wine. Boaz brought some bread to Ruth. "Dip your bread in this refreshing wine." She sat with Boaz and the reapers and ate until she was satisfied. The bread that remained in her portion she tied into the folds of her skirt. When it was time to return to work, the harvesters arose and looked at the silent young woman. Boaz stood over her and said, "Let her glean even among the sheaves, and do not tease this young woman. And pull out some from your bundles for her, and leave them on the ground for her, for her life is hard, and she has come to live among us."

So Ruth gleaned in the field, and her bundle grew heavy with grain. As the sun set at the edge of the field, she beat out what she had gleaned and filled her sack with barley.

When she returned to the small house, Naomi was amazed at the amount of grain she had gleaned. "Who was so generous to us? And where did you glean so much barley?"

"The man was kind and ordered that I be allowed to glean each day of the harvest. His name is Boaz."

Naomi fell to her knees in surprise. "Boaz! Blessed be God, for Boaz has shown us great kindness and has not forsaken either the living or the dead."

"Do you know this man?" Ruth asked, overcome by her mother-in-law's joy. "Do you remember him from the time before you left Bethlehem?"

"He is of the clan of my husband, of Elimelek," Naomi said, running her hands through the mound of grain. "He is a relative of ours, one of our nearest kin."

"It is good that we have returned to Judah," Ruth replied.

"You do as he says, and glean in his fields. Just be sure that you stay close to the young women. I remember well the days of harvest, and the young men's delight in teasing a young woman, especially a foreign woman, with no one to protect her."

"Until the barley and wheat harvest end, I shall glean in the field of Boaz, for he has shown us kindness."

When Ruth returned from the field of Boaz on the final day of harvest, she gave Naomi the grain she had gleaned and some of the bread she had been given that day for her own meal. "The fields are finished, the grain is gathered in, and tonight the harvesters will eat and drink at the threshing floor." She looked at the grain store in the front room of the house. "But what shall we do when this grain is no more?"

Naomi sat on a stool next to her daughter-in-law. "I have thought of this too. And that I must find a suitable husband for you."

"I am content to remain here with you," Ruth said.

"But only with a husband for you will we be able to manage from harvest to harvest. And I have a plan."

Ruth saw that Naomi's face had some of the life that had been drained away when her two sons died. Returning to her homeland, returning to her husband's small house, had helped to restore life to her. And Ruth knew it had been wise to return to Judah with Naomi at the time of the barley harvest.

Naomi leaned forward, her words full of eagerness. "Now this Boaz who has shown you such kindness. Is he not our kin? Is he not going to be winnowing on the threshing floor tonight?"

Ruth nodded. "The celebration has already begun."

"Then this is what you must do. Put on your loveliest robe and make yourself fragrant with perfumes and oils. Then when darkness has fallen, go down to the threshing floor. Wait until Boaz has eaten and drunk his fill. Be sure to see where he lies down to sleep. Then when the wine has made all the harvesters heavy with sleep, quietly make your way to where Boaz lies."

"What if I am seen?"

"Wine after harvest acts like a heavy blanket of sleep. They will know nothing till morning's light. Go and lie next to Boaz."

Ruth held up a violet robe with embroidery around its neck. "Is this the robe?" she smiled.

"And these are the earrings," said Naomi, removing the

gold leafs from her own ears. "Now go, my daughter. Make ready for the night."

As she walked toward the spent fields, Ruth listened to the laughter and merrymaking coming from the threshing floor. She crept close enough to the celebration to see Boaz drinking from the wine skin. Time after time harvesters approached their master and offered him food and wine. And full of merriment he joined in their song. She waited until the torches burned low and the voices grew soft. The harvesters settled down on the floor to sleep under the star-stained sky, and Boaz walked to the end of the heap of grain. He removed his sandals, loosened his robe, and lay down.

Ruth waited until his breathing grew heavy. Then she walked soundlessly over the ground and lay close to Boaz. She felt the warmth of his body as she pressed close to him. She lay next to him in the cool night air and wondered at her own daring.

Suddenly Boaz twitched and gasped and opened his eyes. He looked at the small figure next to him. He reached out his hand. "Who are you?" he said, his voice hoarse with sleep.

Ruth took his hand and whispered, "I am Ruth, the young widow of Mahlon. Spread your cloak of refuge over me, for you are my next of kin."

"Then this is no dream." He smiled at the woman lying close to him. "Bless you for coming to me, instead of to another man, be he young or old, rich or poor. Fear not, my sweet daughter, I will do for you all that you ask, for all the people in Bethlehem know that you are a worthy woman. Now, you may not know that there is a kinsman nearer than I. Stay here with me through this night, and tomorrow, I shall go to him. If he will meet the obligation of redeemer for the field of Naomi, then such is his right.

But if he does not perform the duty, then I, Boaz, will do the part of the next of kin for you. Yes, indeed, dear Ruth, lie down till the first light of morning, and I shall do the part of the next of kin for you tomorrow!"

Ruth stayed with Boaz until streaks of dawn pinkened the sky. Before the light was strong enough for one to recognize another's face, Ruth left the threshing floor. Boaz caught the hem of her garment. "Tell no one that you have come here to me. Now hold out your cloak, dear one."

Ruth held out her garment and Boaz measured into it heaps of barley. They tied the bundle together and Ruth carried it back to the house. Naomi was sitting in the doorway. She ran to meet her daughter-in-law.

"How did it go?"

Ruth told her all that had happened during the night. "And then he arose with me and gave me the grain, and told me that I must not return to you, my mother-in-law, with empty hands."

"He is indeed a good man. For now our grain store is full. I know this man, and he will not rest until he has settled the matter today."

Later that day Boaz went to the city gate, where the men of the town transacted business. Sitting with a few friends was the man Boaz sought. "Hey, come here for a moment, Roly-poly. It is with you that I have business this day." Boaz gathered ten men from the elders of the city, and they all sat down together.

"Naomi, who has returned from the land of Moab, is selling her part of the land, which belonged to our kinsman Elimelek. I thought you should know, since you are the first in line to buy it, Roly-poly." Boaz gestured to the men who were listening. "And these elders of our people can witness your purchase. And I shall act for Naomi."

Boaz waited, but the man said nothing.

Boaz remained patient. "If you will buy the land, then

buy it, but if you do not intend to buy it, let me know. For then I, as next in line, intend to buy it for myself."

The man leaned forward. "Yes, indeed, I shall exercise my right. It is good land and I shall certainly buy it from Naomi."

Boaz waited for a moment. "I almost forgot, Roly-poly, the day one buys the field from Naomi, one also takes Ruth, the widow of Mahlon, son of Naomi and Elimelek, as wife. As is our custom, her son shall inherit the field in order to restore the name of the dead and to preserve his inheritance."

Roly-poly looked at Boaz in surprise. Confounded, he shook his head. "No, no, that is not what I intend! For I would lose the field and hurt the rights of my own dear children. What good would that be to me and mine? Take the right of purchase yourself, and take the widow too, for I renounce all claim to them."

As was the custom in Israel, Roly-poly took off his sandal and gave it to Boaz, as proof of his intention to relinquish his rights as next of kin.

Boaz held the sandal and turned to the elders. "You are witnesses this day that I have bought from the hand of Naomi all that belonged to Elimelek and all that belonged to Chilion and Mahlon. And Ruth, the Moabite woman, I shall take for my wife. And I promise that the name of the dead shall live; his people shall be my people, and his son shall be my son. You are all witnesses to my pledge this day."

The elders gathered around him. "We are indeed witnesses. And may this woman, whom you are bringing into your house, be like Rachel and Leah, and build up the house of Israel. May you prosper and may the Lord give you many children."

So Ruth was married to Boaz and she and Naomi went to live with him. At the time of the following barley harvest, when the fields were once more heavy with grain, Ruth bore a son. The women of the village joined together in celebration of the child.

Naomi greeted them at the door of the house, holding the infant in her arms. The women were joyful. "Blessed be God, who has not left you empty and without children. God has nourished you with food and with this beautiful child."

The women danced and sang. Then one of them stepped forward. "May this child keep you full of delight now and in your old age. May he provide you with sweetness and laughter."

"And blessed be Ruth, who has borne this child for you. She has been more precious to you than seven sons, for you shall not be alone."

Then Naomi kissed the child and laughed in great joy with the women of Bethlehem. It was the women who named the boy Obed. He became the father of Jesse, the father of David, who became king over Israel.

N O T E S

The book of Ruth tells the story of one woman's courage and loyalty to another in a time when a woman's well-being depended on having a husband and sons to care for her. The Hebrew name Naomi means "pleasant," but when Naomi loses her husband and sons, she symbolically changes her name from Naomi to Mara, meaning "bitter." She urges her two daughters-in-law to return to their Moabite families and remarry, because only through marriage will their futures be assured.

When Ruth makes the surprising decision to return with her mother-in-law to Bethlehem, Naomi at first barely acknowledges her presence. Ruth's decision is particularly unexpected since she is a Moabite, and the Moabites were frequently considered Israel's enemies. Her famous speech to Naomi, "Where you go, I will go . . . ," often used in wedding ceremonies, shows that her loyalty to her mother-in-law extends to accepting Naomi's people and her God. Even though Moab was only a few days' journey from the land of Israel, the two nations had separate customs, religion, and food.

Famine was a great threat in ancient Israel, and a few years without a good harvest could destroy whole towns. A famine in Bethlehem (the name in Hebrew means "house of bread") leads Elimelek and his family to leave their own country and settle in Moab, east of the Dead Sea. When Naomi, now a widow, hears that there is again bread in Bethlehem of Judah, she decides to return to her homeland.

The story shows how, through Ruth, Naomi again becomes "full." Boaz marries Ruth, and according to the custom he mentions, the first son she bears to Boaz is considered the son and heir of her dead husband Mahlon. Boaz's faithfulness to the family of Elimelek at the end of the book corresponds to Ruth's faithfulness to Naomi at the beginning. The name of the nearest of kin, who renounces his claim to Elimelek's property and to Ruth, in Hebrew is *peloni almoni,* a vague name, more to do with sound than sense. Some interpreters have called this man "Mr. So-and-so." To capture the humorous nonsensical Hebrew name in English, we have called this character "Roly-poly."

Michal Saves David's Life

*M*ichal sat at the window playing on the lyre her father King Saul had given her as a wedding gift. Her face was bathed in the golden light of the late afternoon. Her eyes scanned the courtyard below, looking for a glimpse of her husband David. Her fingers moved lightly across the strings, and she sang softly to herself.

> *"Let him kiss me with the kisses of his mouth*
> *For his love is sweeter than wine.*
> *Like an apple tree among the trees of the forest*
> *So is my love among the young men."*

She rested the lyre by the window. Saul had given it to her with his blessing, but Michal knew that her father did not like the idea of having his rival for the people's affection as a son-in-law. How fortunate for her that David was able to meet her father's unreasonable bride price. She idly picked up an ivory comb and drew it through her long hair. Would the harshness between David and her father ever end? Rubbing perfumed oil into her temples, she continued,

> *"I will rise and roam the city,*
> *in the squares and in the streets.*
> *I will seek the one I love.*
> *I searched for him but could not find him. . . ."*

Suddenly the door opened and Michal's brother Jonathan burst into the room. "Is our father here?"

"Of course not. He has not come to our house since the night he threw the spear at David, who hadn't done anything to provoke him."

Jonathan looked around impatiently. "We must protect David!"

"David! Why?"

"A great distress has fallen upon our father Saul. He forbade the musicians to play. Brooding by the light of the dying torches, he hurled his spear at the wall, as though to murder the elusive shadows playing there. This morning he threatened to kill David. Hatred closed his ears, and he would not listen to reason. Sometimes I cannot be a son to him." He sat on the bed and covered his face with his hands.

Michal ran to the door and peered outside. "We still have time, Jonathan. There are no soldiers coming from the direction of the king's house."

Jonathan looked out the window. "There is no one in the

fields, either. But we haven't much time. I heard our father planning with one of his soldiers to send men in the night to set a trap for David."

Michal took her brother's arm. "Where is David? Perhaps they have caught him already in the fields. What exactly did you hear? What does the king intend to do?"

"I know for certain he has ordered that David be killed."

Tears filled Michal's eyes. "If he has ordered such a thing, then I must be a wife. I cannot be a daughter."

"I'm going back to the fields to look for my friend. Perhaps I can warn him to stay away until the king's temper cools."

"I'll go with you."

Her brother shook his head. "Stay here in case David returns."

Jonathan did not wait for his sister to reply. Pulling his robe around him, he left, closing the door softly behind him.

Michal watched her brother zigzag past the other houses until he reached the open fields behind them. She thought back to the first time she had seen David. He was so handsome and brave! She had loved him at once. Never had there been such a hero in Israel! All the women had danced and sung with joy before him in the streets after he slew the fearsome Philistine giant Goliath. The army marched behind him laden with Philistine plunder, each soldier as proud as if he had been the one to answer Goliath's challenge for hand-to-hand combat. David had taken his life in his hands that day, and what a great victory he wrought in Israel! Smiling at the cheering crowds, he had looked directly at her. And he had the most glorious eyes she had ever seen.

"My, the king's daughter looks serious this evening." Michal was so deep in thought that she had not heard her husband enter the room.

"Oh, David!" Michal cried out as she threw her arms around his neck. "I was so worried! Jonathan has gone to the fields searching for you! My father has ordered his soldiers to kill you in the morning. If you do not save your life tonight, tomorrow you will be a dead man!"

David looked around the room. Already the shadows of night made pools of darkness in every corner.

"You must escape! There is no time to lose." While David stood still as a statue, Michal hurried around the room. She took a stout rope and tied it securely around the window lattice. She pulled on it until it was fast. "Here, take the end of this rope. I'll let you down through the window. Stay away from the courtyard. Guards will be watching the door. You can hide in the fields."

David slipped out the window, his hands gripping the heavy rope. Before she could tell him what was in her heart, he had crept across the courtyard into the shadows of the night. Soon after he left, a heavy knock came at the door. Her heart in her throat, Michal looked around the room. "I must gain time for David to get away," she thought, clutching her hands together. The knocking grew more insistent.

"Just a moment," she called out. "I'm not dressed." As she spoke, she threw back the covers on the bed. She went over to a corner of the room where a basalt statue of a winged sphinx stood. Grasping it by its pointed ears, she dragged the heavy statue across the room and maneuvered it onto the bed. "I'll need something to make him longer," she muttered to herself.

In another corner was a smaller stone statue of a woman holding a fig leaf. Straining under its weight, Michal carried it over to the bed and placed the smaller statue above the sphinx.

The knocking began again. "Open the door in the name of the king," a voice called.

"Just a moment—I'm coming." Michal grabbed a coverlet of goat's hair and placed it at the head of the statues in the bed, arranging the covers to look as if a person were lying asleep.

Slowly and deliberately Michal unbolted the door and opened it a crack. "What do you want at this hour of the night?" she snapped. "What's so important that it can't wait until the morning? When my father the king hears of this disturbance, you'll regret this intrusion."

A messenger and three armed men stood before her. The messenger was taken aback by Michal's curtness. "I'm sorry to disturb you. But we have orders from King Saul to bring David to him at once."

"That's not possible." Michal opened the door a bit more so that the men could see the bed behind her, with the form in it made up to look like David. "My husband is sick."

The man looked apologetic. "We did not mean to disturb you, my lord." He bowed to the mound in the bed. "We shall inform the king that you cannot come at this time." Michal stood at the door and said nothing. The messenger looked uncomfortable. "I am sorry that we disturbed you," he murmured as he and the men departed. "We were only carrying out King Saul's orders."

Michal closed the door and waited. She smiled as she looked at the statues bundled up in the bed. She patted the goat's hair coverlet. Then she curled up on the bed beside her stone husband and fell asleep.

The sound of knocking startled her. A loud voice rang out in the night. "Open the door in the name of the king!"

"I told you my husband was ill in bed," Michal scowled at the messenger and the guards.

"The king said, 'If David is ill in bed, bring him to me ill in his bed.'" Firmly but politely the man pushed Michal aside. "Grab the other three sides," he said to the guards, "and we'll bring him, bed and all, before the king."

They bent to the bed frame and heaved it up off the floor.

"This is heavier than I thought," the messenger panted.

"We'll try to be careful carrying you down the steps, my lord," one of the guards spoke to the mound.

They had moved the bed a few feet when one of the guards stumbled. He pitched forward, knocking into the figure on the bed. The goat's hair cover fell to the floor at his feet. Startled, the other men dropped the bed. They peered at the headless mound lying at their feet.

"What have we here?"

"There is something peculiar in this bed," one of the guards exclaimed. He snatched off the covers, revealing the statues lumped together on the bed.

"David has fled!"

"We must report to the king!"

The king's men rushed from the room, leaving Michal with her ruse.

"My father won't sleep at all this night," she thought. "David must have had time to reach safety by now. My plan has worked." She picked up her embroidery and wondered how long it would be before she saw her husband again.

Before too long a great clatter was heard at the front of the house. Almost immediately Saul and his soldiers entered the room. "Why have you deceived me and let my enemy escape?" With the pointed end of his spear King Saul poked through the pile of bedclothes.

Michal approached her father. "He threatened to kill me if I didn't let him go." She shook out one of the crumpled covers and began to fold it. "I was afraid. I did not know what to do."

"You should have come to me."

"There was no time, Father."

King Saul shook his head. "But you helped him," he shouted, his face red with anger. "You gave him time to escape my soldiers."

Michal ran her hand over the cool stone of the sphinx. "He is gone now."

Saul set one of the statues on the floor. "He may have escaped my soldiers this night, but I will hunt him down." Still in a rage King Saul stormed out of David's house. His soldiers moved the empty bed back to its place and left.

Walking to the window, Michal looked out at the black night. David would have to keep running. But David was quick and cunning. He would not be defeated.

> *"Flee, my love,*
> *be like a gazelle or young hart*
> *Upon the mountains of spices."*

Sighing, she picked up her lyre. When would David return? When would she see her love again?

N O T E S

The story of Michal's planning David's dramatic escape when Saul seeks to kill him comes from the first book of Samuel, chapter 19. Michal does not see David again until much later, after her father King Saul and her brother Jonathan have been killed in battle against the Philistines and David has become king over the tribe of Judah in the South. During his days as a fugitive from Saul, David took two more wives, Ahinoam and Abigail. In order to prevent David from making any claim to the throne through his daughter Michal, Saul married her to another man, Paltiel.

When David has designs on the northern part of Saul's former kingdom, he demands the return of his wife Michal from Saul's son Ishbosheth, who rules the northern tribes. Their reunion is not described. We meet Michal again in 2 Samuel 6, where she criticizes David's behavior as he leads the procession that brings the ark of the Lord into Jerusalem. The biblical story says that her love, so vividly illustrated in the story we tell here, had turned to hatred. We may assume her bitterness is the result of David's lack of interest in her. David responds to Michal's criticism with a biting rebuke, and the story ends with the words, "Michal, Saul's daughter, had no child to the day of her death." This, then, is the fate of the woman who once risked her life to save David.

We know very little about the objects Michal uses as disguises in David's bed. Some scholars think they were household gods; in Genesis 31, they seem to have some connection to inheritance rights.

The verses that Michal sings to herself we have taken from the Song of Songs, the Bible's supreme example of love poetry. David was brought to Saul's court to play the lyre in order to soothe the troubled king (1 Samuel 16:16–23); in our story Michal plays the lyre. A lyre such as Michal might have played is pictured on a seal, dating from the seventh century B.C.E., that bears the inscription, "(Belonging) to Maadanah, the king's daughter." Nothing more is known of this woman, nor is her father identified. She probably chose the lyre as her emblem on her seal because she played the instrument; we thus found it appropriate that Michal, the king's daughter, should play the lyre.

Abigail, the Wife More Precious than Jewels

"They say he is the richest man in all Judah," Abigail said, looking out the window to where the donkeys of Nabal of Maon grazed in the sun. His servants waited patiently for their master, standing beside animals loaded with gifts for the family of the young woman he hoped to make his bride. For an hour the stranger had been talking with the father of Abigail, known as the most beautiful girl of marriageable age in Judah.

"But will this husband be good and kind?" wondered Abigail's sister Leah. In two years time it would be her turn to leave her father's house and marry a nearby landowner.

"It is the woman's place to be kind and manage the

household," Abigail reminded her. "A good wife is more precious than jewels, and nothing a man desires can compare with her. Long life is in her right hand; in her left hand are riches and honor."

Shoshannah, the youngest sister, burst into laughter. "Marry this Calebite and you will have three thousand sheep in your left hand." She tugged at her sister's silk robe. "A hillside of perfume won't kill the smell of three thousand sheep."

"A foolish woman is noisy and knows no shame," Abigail warned her.

Leah wound a flower into Abigail's hair. "You must go to Mother and wait to be summoned to meet Nabal. And do not wonder about his goodness. Surely this man's wealth comes from walking in God's righteousness."

Shoshannah kissed her sister. "Sometimes I allow my tongue to dance to the music of nonsense. Forgive me, dear Abigail. They have weighed many offers of marriage this year and would not marry you to a fool. And it is indeed fitting that a bride as clever and beautiful as you should manage a great household. It is what Mother has trained us for."

Abigail went to the room where her mother sat in front of her open jewel chest. "Come here, my daughter. I wish to give you this necklace, which my mother fastened around my neck the day I left my parents' house to build a life with your father."

"Then it is to be this Nabal." Abigail looked anxiously at her mother. "Father would not be swayed by his wealth?"

"Abigail, have we taught you so little?" Her mother embraced her gently. "Whoever trusts in riches will wither—"

"But the righteous will flourish like a green leaf," finished her daughter. "I will trust in the Lord and in the wisdom of my father."

A few days later Abigail rode off with her new husband.

Her sisters watched from the window until the donkeys had disappeared from view.

Nabal presented his bride with an ornately carved silver comb. "Your teeth are like a flock of sheep that have just been washed. Each one has its twin. Your lips are like a scarlet thread, and your mouth is lovely."

"You have given me many gifts, my husband, and I shall try to be worthy of you."

Abigail was true to her word. As the months turned to years, she gained the respect of all the servants. For she treated them fairly and showed concern for them and for their families. She rose early in the morning, while it seemed still to be night. No one worked harder than Abigail. And at their work in the house and in the fields the servants spoke of their mistress with honor.

> *"She puts her hand to the distaff*
> *and her hands hold the spindle.*
> *She opens her hands to the poor*
> *and reaches out her hands to the needy.*
> *She makes herself fine clothing of purple and saffron.*
> *She looks to the needs of her household*
> *and does not eat of the bread of idleness."*

But as much as Abigail was beloved and seemed to bring the bloom to the flowers in the fields, Nabal was known as a churl, coarse as the unwashed wool of the sheep. He drank strong drink and fell into a beery sleep each night. He roamed the hills with his sheepshearers and was feared by his neighbors. "A strutting cock will soon fall," the men whispered. "A man's pride will bring him low," their wives agreed. But Nabal's wealth increased. "Will no one ever bring that man to his knees?" the people wondered.

Nabal was preparing to ride out to the hills where the summer sheepshearing was taking place. "Gather provisions for my journey. Wineskins and meat and loaves for me and for my men," he ordered his wife.

"She opens her mouth with wisdom and the teaching of kindness is on her tongue," the servants said behind their hands as their despised master rode into the wilderness with his steward. "But his words are knives, ready to devour the poor from off the earth."

Now David and his band of men had been camped for several months in the wilderness near Carmel. Hiding in the caves in the hills near Judah, fleeing from the jealous wrath of King Saul, waiting until the time when God chose to proclaim him king, David outwitted his royal enemy. With the help of Michal, his wife, David had escaped the murderous rage of her father the king and fled to the wilderness. Meeting secretly in the drought-dry hills of Ziph, Jonathan had sworn allegiance to David. "Do not be afraid. My father Saul will never lay a hand upon you. Even he knows that you will rule over Israel someday, and I shall be your second in command."

David called ten of his bravest young men. They knew that Nabal, the wealthiest landowner in the hill country, was shearing his sheep. "Go up to Carmel, and when you come to Nabal, greet him in my name. You know the words, 'May you have peace. May your household have peace.' Tell him that some of his shepherds have been on the same hillsides as our men, and we have raised no hand against them. Tell Nabal to count his sheep, and he will see that we have not slipped one solitary lamb from its fold. And when he has agreed that we have treated him well, tell him that it is just and proper for him to look upon us with favor at this special time of sheepshearing."

Abishai stepped forward. Ruddy and almost as handsome as David, Abishai was the same age David had been when he smote the Philistine giant Goliath in the Valley of the Terebinth.

"Yes, for the hillsides are empty of food," Abishai said. He eyed Goliath's sword, which now hung from David's hip. "And were it not for our righteousness, Nabal's lambs would have filled our bellies instead of his pens."

David laughed. "He will be no match for your clever words, Abishai."

When the young men went and spoke fine words to Nabal in the name of David, the landowner sneered. "Who is this David to me? The son of Jesse is now one to reckon with? Throughout the hills one hears of servants breaking away from their masters. It is not cause for respect, but for laughter."

"Were it not for our righteousness—" began one of the young men.

Nabal interrupted him. "Shall I take bread and wine and meat meant for my own sheepshearers and give such fine food to bandits hiding in caves?"

When David heard of Nabal's answer, he was filled with anger. "Let everyone strap on his sword," David shouted to his men. "Nabal will know before the lamps of night are lit that the son of Jesse is indeed one to reckon with." Four hundred men rode out with David, and two hundred stayed behind to guard the camp. David's anger gathered speed as they rode down the mountainside. "By my life, when the light of morning spreads across this mountain, not one man of Nabal's household will be left alive!"

Meanwhile, Nabal's servants went to Abigail and told her what had happened. "David sent messengers from the wilderness to salute our master, and very politely did they request some wine and bread and meat. He raged at them and treated them like ravens pecking at the harvest grain."

"Who are these men?" asked Abigail, her voice low and steady.

"They were good to us and we lost nothing all the time we were shepherding near them. They were like a wall surrounding us, day and night, and no one in those hills dared harm us or our master's sheep."

Another of the servants bowed and clutched the hem of Abigail's gown. "At any moment David will send misfortune to clothe us and all this house. For our master cannot be made to hear reason. And we are in great danger."

Abigail listened to their words and saw the look of fear on each of their faces. "Gather up two hundred loaves, two skins of wine, five dressed sheep, five loads of raisins, and load them on the donkeys," she commanded them. "I will ride out with you to the place where David is encamped." Throwing her cloak over her shoulders, she mounted her donkey and rode down the mountain. She spoke no word to Nabal. She told him nothing of her plan.

Within hours Abigail and her servants met up with David and his men, whose swords were gleaming in the sunlight. She reined in her donkey and got down on the ground and bowed at David's feet. "Please, my lord, listen for a moment to the words of your humble servant. Pay no attention to the words of the foolish Nabal. For as his name means 'fool,' so does his nature bark and snarl. If only your men had asked to speak to me. To make amends for the rudeness of my husband, I have brought to you and your good men all that you have asked for and more."

David looked into her guileless eyes, clear as a spring-fed brook. His anger began to melt at the sight of her delicate face. He took the bread she offered but found his mouth empty of words.

"Please, my lord, by the living God you have been restrained from committing bloodguilt. Do not let the blood of the foolish Nabal be upon your hands. Empty your hands of vengeance, and pay no heed to those of your enemies like Nabal, who would wish harm to my lord David."

Her words played around him like the melody of a lyre.

"I pray that you will forgive the trespass of your humble

servant Abigail. Accept these small presents that I offer to you and go in peace. For the Lord God will certainly make my lord David a strong house because you are fighting the battles of the Lord God. Do not let evil be found near you all the days of your life.''

David's men took the sacks of bread and raisins that Abigail's servants held out. He could not take his eyes from the lovely woman, who continued to speak as though no servants or soldiers surrounded them. ''If men rise up to do evil and threaten your life, the Lord your God will protect your life as a mother protects her infant wrapped in a warm bundle. For the Lord God shall proclaim you prince over all Israel, and then you shall have no cause for grief or pain. No enemy shall come at you, as a stone shot from the hollow of a sling.''

David stared at her intently. What an extraordinary woman, who spoke with the tongue of a prophet. Not since he had visited Samuel in Ramah had he felt the will of God surround him with such power. ''Blessed be the Lord God of Israel for sending you to meet me this day!''

''And when the Lord has indeed dealt well with you, my lord, please remember your servant.''

''Blessed are you, who have kept me from bloodguilt and from avenging myself with my own hand.'' David raised his sword in the air and held it aloft while Abigail and her men rode back up the mountain path to Carmel.

When they reached the house, night had fallen. Nabal and his men were feasting in the courtyard. The smell of wine was heavy in the air. ''Well, the great Abigail has graced us with her presence,'' said her husband, his hand overturning a goblet. He lifted the silver goblet and held it wavering in the air. ''Shall you stop and have a glass with us?''

Abigail said nothing. The coldness of her glance was not noticed by the drunken men. The next morning, after she had seen to the grinding of the grain for the day, she went to the courtyard, where Nabal had snored away the night. The wine had left him and he lay limp and flaccid in sleep.

"I have stopped the sword of David from entering your belly," she said quietly. "I have saved the lives of the men who watch our sheep because of the bravery of those who rode out with me."

A choked scream low in his throat, like that of an animal caught in a trap, filled the air. And then, staring sightlessly, Nabal lay on the ground unblinking. For ten days he did not move. He could not see or hear those of his household moving around him. He lay like a stone until the Lord God took back his life. Nabal was not mourned by his wife or his men. They continued the work of the household, pasturing the flocks and carding the wool. Life went on as though the master of the house were off in the hills, visiting his shepherds. Abigail hummed at her loom, content in her life.

When word reached David that Nabal had been struck dead, he rejoiced. "Blessed be God who has avenged the insult that I suffered at the hand of that cur. Blessed be God, who has held me back from evil, and blessed be Abigail, whose words stilled my hand upon the hilt of my sword!"

Within days he ordered his men to Carmel to speak with Abigail, Nabal's widow. "Our master David has sent us to take you to his place in the hills to become his wife." Abigail was not surprised to see them. "It is better to be married to a king than to be a fool's wife," she said as she arranged with her female servants to accompany her.

The next morning she and her servants rode out while the morning chill still lay on the air. "It is well that all these lands shall come to David and that I shall be with him when the Lord makes him prince over Israel."

NOTES

The biblical story of Abigail begins with the announcement of the death of the prophet Samuel. Her prophecy to David that "the Lord will certainly make my lord a sure house . . . and appoint you prince over Israel" anticipates the prophecy later delivered by Nathan. Abigail thus serves as a prophetic link between two great monarchic prophets, Samuel and Nathan.

Our story follows the characterization of the biblical story-teller, who emphasizes Abigail's goodness and temperance. She is the perfect example of the "good wife, more precious than jewels" described in the book of Proverbs. Since proverbs may have been popular with upper-class families at the time our story is set, the tenth century B.C.E., Abigail and her sisters and servants recite proverbs.

The story contrasts the wealthy lout Nabal with the quick-thinking woman who saves the sheepshearers from David's wrath. At the same time she protects David from bloodguilt and reminds him that life and death are the province of God. The story of Abigail is placed between two accounts of David's sparing Saul's life in the book of Samuel. The words of the brave and daring prophet Abigail underscore both for David and for the reader that David must not act to hasten his ascent to the throne, but rather wait for God to achieve this goal for him.

Abigail's lengthy speech is a striking example of the power of words in the Bible. The Hebrew name Nabal means fool; the man is a Calebite and *caleb* means dog. Thus when Abigail ridicules her husband to David, she is presenting a double pun: one on her husband's name and one on the name of his tribe.

The Wise Woman of Tekoa
and the Wise Woman of Abel

From time to time during the reign of King David, there arose a wise woman to give guidance and counsel to the king and his people. These were not stable times, for although David's accomplishments were many, his reign was not peaceful. Two women whose voices of wisdom and moderation soothed the king and may well have altered the direction of his rule were the wise woman from Tekoa and the wise woman from Abel of Beth-maacah.

Joab, David's general, sought out the wise woman of Tekoa when he saw how David longed to see his son Absalom again. Three years earlier, to avenge the rape of his sister Tamar, Absalom had killed his half brother Amnon and fled the kingdom. In the council room and in the palace court, David grieved for his son. But he refused to be comforted. In spite of the pleas of his advisers and courtiers, King David would not permit Absalom to return. As the months turned to years, the smile left the king's face. He could no longer listen to music.

Seeing how deeply David grieved over his son, Joab devised a plan. The king had not heeded any of Joab's supplications to bring Absalom back to Jerusalem. "He will not listen to me," Joab thought, "but there is one who may be able to ease the king's heart. Her words are said to play like music on a troubled soul." After he had refined his plan, Joab summoned his most trusted messenger. "Go to Tekoa and seek out the wise woman who lives there. Bring her to Jerusalem at once."

The next afternoon the messenger returned with the woman and brought her before Joab. "The king is so distressed over his son that he is neglecting his duties," Joab said, peering into the woman's kind eyes. "I need your help to convince him that his anger has burned long enough. It is time to bring Absalom back. My plan is simple. Pretend that you are in mourning. Put on mourners' garments, do not anoint yourself with oil, and unbind your hair as if you have been mourning for many days. Present the king with a petition for judgment. Say that you too have lost a son—"

"I will know what to say when I am before the king. If words are to come from the heart, they cannot be pronounced beforehand."

"Of course the words shall be your own," Joab said apologetically.

"I will do as you say, my lord Joab, for all Israel knows of the king's grief, and all Israel longs for Absalom's return. I will find the words to make the king understand the right thing to do."

Joab arranged for the wise woman to have an audience

with the king the next day. When she came before King
David, she bowed to the ground. "Help me, O wise King
David. Hear the plea of your saddened servant for justice."
Her anguished voice cut through the king's musings.

"What is your trouble?" The king's voice showed his lack
of interest.

Seeing that her disarrayed garments had not affected
the man, the wise woman clasped her hands in front of
him. "Alas, O King. I am a widow. My husband is dead.
I had two sons, but they quarreled one day in the field.
They came to blows, and since no one else was there to
separate them, one of them killed the other. Now my relatives cry for the blood of the murderer to avenge the
dead! What am I to do, O King? For I have only this
son. He is the sole heir, and if they kill him, no one will
be left to keep alive my husband's name."

"Though he is guilty of killing his brother, he must not
be killed," said the king, "for that would leave you without
an inheritance in Israel. Return to your house." King
David waved his hand toward the door. "I will give orders
concerning you, so that no harm will come to your son."

Finally the king was listening closely to the wise woman's
story. "Let the king call upon the name of the Lord our
God," she said softly, "that no one shall harm my son, for
they all seek his life."

David looked straight at the woman. "As the Lord lives,
not one hair of his head shall fall to the ground."

"May I speak another word before the king?" The woman
spoke leisurely, as though she and the king had just shared
a meal across a small table.

His face came alive with interest. "Speak."

The wise woman of Tekoa took a deep breath. In speaking
with Joab, she had thought the task sounded simple. "I
have laid my case before the king because the king is wise,
like an angel of God, able to discern what is right. I knew

your word would set me at rest and preserve the life of my son." She stepped forward until she was an arm's length from the throne. "Consider, my lord, that in giving this decision, the king convicts himself. You have banished your son, and deprived yourself of his presence. Shall you refuse to bring him home when your heart calls to him? Why have you planned such a thing to hurt yourself and punish the people of Israel?"

David's eyes grew wide with amazement. "Tell me,"—he scowled at the woman—"is Joab behind this?"

"Indeed, my lord, Joab is a good man and told me of the king's trouble. The king has wisdom like an angel of God for feeling the troubles of his people. Joab did send me here in hopes that a mother's grief would remind the king of his own. There was no evil planned against the king, but rather the deepest desire to bring about your son's return."

The king's head sank low upon his chest. For several moments he did not speak. "Bring Joab here!" the king said softly. The wise woman could barely hear the king's voice from where she stood. The attendants approached closer. "Bring Joab to me," King David repeated.

Looking at the wise woman as though to read success or failure upon her face, Joab entered the council chamber. David rose from his throne and went forward to meet his general. "I accept the lesson this woman has taught me. You chose well in sending her to me. You may go and bring young Absalom to the palace."

Joab bowed before the king and blessed him. "Today I know that God has blessed us in the wisdom of this woman from Tekoa. Through her I have found favor in your eyes, my lord the king. With a light heart I go to bring Absalom back to the king." Joab bowed again as he left the king's presence.

David smiled at the woman from Tekoa. "May the Lord

bless you for your words of wisdom. May your wisdom increase and be known throughout Israel."

"May God bless the king in all his thoughts and deeds. And through King David may the kingdom of Israel flourish." Bowing deeply, she left David's presence and went home to Tekoa.

As Joab journeyed toward Geshur, where Absalom had taken refuge in the land of his mother's father, he wondered how Absalom would react to the news that his father was willing for him to return to the court. Now that the king would be reconciled to his son, perhaps the fortunes of the kingdom would increase. But Joab's hopes for a better future were not to be fulfilled.

By the time Absalom returned to Jerusalem, David had hardened his heart again. He refused to see Absalom for two more years. When the reunion finally took place, David did not show his son the love he had once given so freely. Absalom, resentful of the way his father treated him and unhappy with the way his father governed the land, led a revolt that almost succeeded.

A worthless fellow named Sheba, from the tribe of Benjamin, took up Absalom's call for rebellion, and people from the northern tribes supported him. Joab and his troops chased Sheba and his followers to the town of Abel of Bethmaacah. Joab directed his soldiers to pack down a ramp with earth, wood, and stones. When they had finished casting up the siege mound against the massive city walls, they began assaulting the wall with a battering ram. The townspeople looked down from the ramparts. "Our city will be destroyed," they lamented. "Joab's forces have us shut up like birds in a cage. What shall we do?"

"Let us consult the wise woman of Abel," someone suggested. "She has helped us out of difficulty more than once."

"Yes, she will know what course to take."

They went to the quarter of the town where the wise woman lived and urged her to come and speak to the king's general. Before she could gather her cloak around her, they had hurried her from the house. Pushing and shouting, they made their way through the crowd, leading the woman to the wall. "Make way, make way, we've brought the wise woman of Abel to tell us how to stop the attack."

The woman peered down from the wall at the siege works and the soldiers below. She squinted against the sunlight as she surveyed Joab's army arrayed before the city wall. "Hear, hear," she called out in a strong voice, "tell Joab to come here. I want to speak with him."

"What do you have to say to the general of King David's army, old woman?" one of the foot soldiers jeered. Several men laughed and pointed their spears toward the gray head above them.

"What I have to say will end this trouble before many young men of the town of Abel lie slaughtered in the sun."

"My lord Joab," cried one of the soldiers, "the wise woman wants to speak with you." The laughter had stopped. "She wants to offer a plan."

Joab drew near to the wall and looked up at the stern face whose features he could barely discern. The crowd was hushed. Everyone's attention was focused on the old woman who spoke so boldly.

"Are you Joab?" the woman called down.

"I am."

"Then listen, General, to what your servant has to say. This city is known near and far for its wisdom. Have you not heard the saying, 'If it's counsel you seek, go to Abel'? As for me, I am a peaceable woman, and I dwell among a faithful people. Why do you want to destroy a city so important to Israel? Would you thus swallow up the Lord's heritage?"

Joab handed his shield and spear to his armor bearer. "Far be it from me that I should want to destroy such a city! It is not true that I desire bloodshed. I seek only the life of Sheba, a man from the hill country of Ephraim, who has lifted up his hand against King David. Give him over to me, and I shall withdraw my troops from the city."

"It shall be as you ask," the woman said. "Before the day is over, his head shall be thrown down to you over the wall. Then you must leave us in peace."

Joab, the general of King David, saluted the woman. "It shall be as you have suggested. The head of the evil Sheba shall allow peace to live in your town."

The woman called for the townspeople to assemble at the city gate. "Listen, citizens of Abel," she cried. "Sheba, a man from the hill country of Ephraim, led a revolt against King David. When he saw that his followers could not prevail against the king's forces, he came to Abel for refuge. Now his presence here endangers us all. If we do not give this rebel over to them, we will be destroyed. I have promised Joab, the king's general, that Sheba's head will be thrown down to him over the wall. In return he will withdraw from the city. Consider, then, whether you will act according to my words or not."

"Throw the rebel down," came a voice from the crowd.

"Off with his head!"

"What is Sheba to us? Why should we all die for his treason?"

The crowd went to the house where Sheba was hiding and dragged him into the street. A few minutes later several young men paraded through the streets carrying the bloodied head of Sheba. "Here is the head of the man you seek," they yelled to Joab as they threw the head over the city wall.

Joab jumped back as the bloody mass hit the ground near his feet. "You have acted wisely," he said, and he gave orders that the trumpet be blown and the soldiers return, each man to his own home. For many years the people of Abel told the tale of the wise woman who had saved the town from the armies of the king.

N O T E S

The stories of the two wise women form part of the story of King David's reign over a united Israel and Judah. Although David's accomplishments were many—for example, he conquered Jerusalem and made it his capital, he brought the ark of the Lord to Jerusalem, and he extended the borders of his kingdom—his reign was filled with problems. Two revolts threatened to divide his kingdom. First his son Absalom led a popular uprising; the revolt was put down and Absalom was killed. Following on the heels of Absalom's rebellion, a Benjaminite named Sheba, from the tribe of the former king, Saul, led a revolt of the northern tribes. This revolt also failed.

In the story of the woman from Tekoa we are told that Joab put words in her mouth, but whether or not he provided her with the details of her fictitious case is open to question. In any event, the woman has to adapt her story to the king's responses, and she manipulates him with flattering words about his wisdom. She begins her false tale with great humility, but holds her own in the following verbal duel with King David. Although her story arouses the king's suspicions, the ruse succeeds and Absalom is restored. The voice of the wise woman from Abel rings out with great authority that is not questioned either by her own townspeople or by the king's general Joab. It is indeed a dramatic moment in biblical storytelling when the words of a wise woman stop the siege of her city.

Wisdom in the book of Proverbs is portrayed as a woman. She is described as originating with God and is associated with creation. The role of the mother in Proverbs is not as the one who bears the children, but rather as the one who nurtures and educates them. The personification of wisdom as a female is an important cultural expression of the primary role of women in the educative process.

In Jewish tradition the female figure of wisdom is sometimes connected with the *shekinah,* a mystical presence or spirit connected directly to God. Like the female wisdom figure in the book of Proverbs, the *shekinah* was with God before creation. It was under her wings that the people of Israel sought the protection of God. The phrase, "The earth did shine with God's glory," was understood by the rabbis to refer to the face of the *shekinah.*

Esther

*M*any years ago King Ahasuerus ruled the Persian Empire, which stretched from India in the East to Ethiopia in the West and contained one hundred twenty-seven provinces. From his fortress at Susa, King Ahasuerus issued edicts and entertained lavishly. An invitation to one of his royal banquets was highly prized. In the third year of his reign he decreed that a banquet would be held for his entire court, all the military officers of the Persian and Median troops, the governors of the provinces, and all who served at his court. The festivities went on for one hundred and eighty days, and the king sent messengers throughout the country ordering that the people be given holidays from their labors and that they hold small celebrations for many days in each province to honor him and his reign.

The king was delighted, for the celebration gave him the opportunity to display the riches and magnificence of his kingdom. Wine flowed unceasingly from golden goblets, no two of them alike, and the fifty thousand guests, wrapped in splendid garments of brilliant colors, trimmed in gold and silver, ate and drank and amused the king inside various courtyard gardens.

The garden nearest the king's chambers was planted with trees bearing delicious fruits and redolent spices. The lower tree trunks were overlaid with pure gold set with inlays of precious stones: jasper, carnelian, and lapis lazuli. The courtiers sat on opulent couches of gold with silver legs, in the shade of the trees that arched high overhead. Yellow-and-white marble pillars supported brightly colored cloths, dyed in brilliant sapphire, green, and cerulean-colored linen, secured with silver rings.

Having enjoyed this banquet every day of the one hundred eighty days it was held, King Ahasuerus gave a second banquet to last seven days for all the men of Susa, the royal capital. At the same time Queen Vashti entertained the women of Susa in her own apartments. On the seventh evening of the banquet, after six days of full cups and lavish drinking, King Ahasuerus sent to the women's quarters for Queen Vashti. He ordered his messengers, "Tell the queen to come immediately to the banquet hall, crowned with her royal diadem, and amuse us. I want all my courtiers to admire my beautiful wife. The most exquisite woman in the world belongs to the king of Persia. It's the law!" he exclaimed, raising his golden goblet.

The messengers hurried through the palace to the queen's apartments, where a much more stately banquet was in progress. The women were telling stories and embroidering fine garments. Several musicians played the queen's favor-

ite melodies on their lyres. Platters of delicacies and sweetmeats were on every table, and the hall rang out with laughter as the women delighted one another with wit and humor.

The messenger bowed low before the queen. "The king
commands that you come to the royal banquet hall, dressed
in the royal diadem, to amuse his royal guests."

"His drunken friends," murmured the woman seated
nearest the queen.

"Tell the king that Queen Vashti does not appear before
drunken courtiers. The queen refuses his invitation."

"It is a command," the messenger said, his eyes fixed on
the marble floor.

"The king will be angry," one of the women said. "Perhaps—"

"The king has been angry before."

"The queen knows how to cool his anger," another woman
said, laughing.

But when the king heard that Queen Vashti refused to
obey him, he threw his cup on the floor, splattering wine on
his attendants' robes. "Tell her she must come," he grum-
bled. "Tell her I have decreed that she come."

"This situation is very serious, my lord." One of his ministers began to pace the floor. "The queen has done a terrible thing. Tonight your kingdom has been shaken by the
voice of a woman."

"It's merely the voice of Queen Vashti," the king said,
his face growing unhappy.

"This situation is indeed very serious." Another courtier
joined the first and paced in front of the king's throne.
"What if our wives hear what your wife has said, and they
refuse to obey our commands?"

A third courtier, a commander of the Median forces,
jumped up. "Then the wives of the army officers will lie on
their couches and ignore the words of their husbands."

"And then the wives of the governors of the one hundred

twenty-seven provinces will say with one voice, 'King Ahasuerus himself commanded Queen Vashti to appear before him and she did not come. We will not serve our husbands either.' Then the ladies of the provincial courts will imitate them, and before the sun has set on this banquet feast, all the women of the entire Persian kingdom will refuse to obey when they are summoned by their husbands. So you see, my lord, this is most certainly very serious."

The king arose from his throne. "King Ahasuerus decrees that Queen Vashti will never again be brought before him." The king looked around the hall at his friends with a questioning expression.

"Excellent, my lord," they agreed.

One of the king's most valued advisers arose. "Let the decree state that the king will confer the royal dignity of queen on another, lovelier woman, who will be worthy to be his queen. And let the decree clearly state that all the women in the kingdom, of high rank and of low, will now bow to the authority of their husbands and obey their every word."

The men of the king's court applauded, and he was pleased. The decree must surely be a good thing. Letters were dispatched to every province of the kingdom, to each province in its own script and to each nation in its own language, guaranteeing that every husband was master in his own house.

A few days later, when the men of the court had returned to their homes to test the decree, the king lay on his couch, all alone except for the attendants who fanned him with the large peacock fans that he favored. He missed Queen Vashti and thought of all the stories that she knew to make him laugh and wished he had not been forced to send her away. "It is time for a fresh young wife," he cried. "Get my ministers," he shouted to the servants who stood just behind those wielding the fans.

"Summon commissioners from each province. They must
search out the loveliest young women and bring them here
to the palace. Then I can choose for myself another wife,
and the royal diadem shall once again be worn by the
most beautiful head in the kingdom."

The king's orders were carried out that very day, and in
every province young women were collected and brought to
the royal palace, where eunuchs guarded them. Before the
month was out, the four hundred most beautiful women in
the empire filled the seraglio. They spent their days apply-
ing ointments and unguents and perfuming themselves.
Each one looked at the others and wondered if she would be
chosen to wear the royal diadem.

The young women learned to pluck the strings of the lyre
while singing the songs that most delighted the king; their
faces were carefully shaded from the scorching sun with
silk-tasseled parasols held over them by the eunuchs of the
seraglio; they soaked for hours in tubs of warm scented
water, and their bodies were rubbed with perfumed oils.
For twelve months the young women were given every ex-
otic beauty treatment known to the Persian court so that
they might be pleasing to King Ahasuerus.

Among the selected maidens of the seraglio was Esther,
the niece and adopted daughter of Mordecai, a Jew from
the tribe of Benjamin and an official of the palace. When
she had been brought to the seraglio, she was so cheerful
and full of fun that she quickly became the favorite of
the attendants. They brought her jars of the best ointments and spices. They carried messages to her from her
uncle Mordecai, who spent his days walking in the gardens surrounding the women's quarters. Because Esther
freely shared her lotions and oil of myrrh with all the
other women, they vied for the privilege of being her companion on walks. Esther was soon the most popular young
woman in the seraglio and shared confidences with all the

others, but she obeyed her uncle Mordecai and never spoke of her origins or her people.

Finally it was time for the young women to be brought into the presence of King Ahasuerus. Each day one of them was chosen and brought by the chief of the eunuchs to the king. On the day that it was Esther's turn, dozens of attendants helped her bathe in water scented with myrtle, her name flower, and dressed her hair with silk ribbons and jewels. Her robe of finest linen was embroidered with threads of red and orange, yellow and blue. Layers of silk fringes fell from her shoulders to her ankles so that she shimmered when she walked.

Her eyes counted the onyx-and-marble tiles that patterned the hallway to the king's chamber, and her heart raced as she approached the huge carved door guarded by the king's sentries. She repeated to herself the king's edict, "Whoever most pleases the king will take Vashti's place as queen."

The door was thrown open, and she was led forward to be inspected by the king. She looked at him from the corner of her eye. He was seated on a throne elaborately decorated with magical figures, their arms raised as if supporting a heavy burden. A marvelous tasseled footstool in the shape of a fearsome lion caught Esther's attention. The king was wearing a garment interwoven with gold and precious stones that glittered when they caught the light. It made him seem frightening, and Esther's knees trembled. She swayed, and the king rushed from his throne to catch her.

"You are the loveliest of all the young women who have tried to amuse me," he said tenderly to her. "Now that you are here, little anemone, my life will be full of sunlight."

Delighted that he had finally found his queen, King Ahasuerus called for the royal diadem and set it upon Esther's head. At a royal banquet attended by more than ten thousand guests, the king proclaimed that Esther was now his queen. The people cheered her, and the courtiers brought little silver gifts to please her.

Mordecai celebrated with the rest of the court and once again warned Esther not to divulge her Jewishness to the king or to any of the Persian courtiers. Shortly after Esther had become queen, Mordecai uncovered a diabolical plot of several of the Guards of the King's Threshold to assassinate King Ahasuerus. Immediately he went to his niece and revealed the plot and the names of the guilty men.

"Perhaps the king will reward me and make me keeper of his royal seal," Mordecai said to Esther. "Having uncovered this villainous crime, I shall be the most important man at court."

When the king heard of the plot to kill him, he had the conspirators sent to the gallows. And like all important events in the Persian court, the matter was recorded in the official Annals of the Reign of Ahasuerus.

Mordecai presented himself to the king each day, in hopes of receiving his reward. But the king never even spoke to him. He drank wine with his favorite courtiers and listened to the music played by the women of the seraglio and issued edicts and planned banquets, but he did not elevate Mordecai. Mordecai wondered if the king was ever going to remember that he had saved his life. Then one day Ahasuerus called together all the palace officials.

"I have decided today to promote one of you over all the others."

Mordecai straightened his robe and prepared to step forward.

"I shall grant this man precedence over all those who administer the king's affairs at court. He shall be keeper of the royal seal, and all edicts will go through his hands."

The king extended his hand and as a symbol of the power being given to him offered the signet ring to Haman, a descendant of the family of Agag. All the men of the court, except Mordecai bowed low in front of the new chief minister. Angry and offended, he left the king's chamber. "By right this honor is mine. Never will I bow to that man. Never will I show him the respect due only to God."

Day after day Mordecai sat in the king's gate and refused to bow when Haman passed by. The other courtiers laughed at the stubbornness of Mordecai. But Haman was not amused. "I shall pay back that arrogant Mordecai. It is not enough to get rid of him alone. If it is true that he is a Jew, then I shall wipe out all the members of Mordecai's race living anywhere in King Ahasuerus' empire. I shall issue a decree of destruction against the Jews, and from this decree they shall learn who is the most important man in this kingdom."

Haman reviewed his plan carefully before revealing it to the king. "There is a group of people who live scattered throughout the nations of your kingdom and who obey their own laws, and eat their own foods, and ignore the decrees issued by your lordship. It pains me to say this, but it is not in the interest of the kingdom to tolerate them any longer. If your lordship will sign this decree to destroy them, I shall pay ten thousand talents of silver into the royal treasury to make up for the taxes you will lose."

The king took his signet ring off his hand and gave it to Haman. "Do what you like with these people, and keep your money also."

Haman lost no time in writing out the orders from the king to the governors of all one hundred twenty-seven provinces to slaughter every Jew—men, women, and children, young and old. The day of the slaughter was determined by casting the *pur,* and the lot fell on the thirteenth day of the twelfth month. Runners were sent carrying copies of the decree to each province in its own script and to each nation in its own language.

When Mordecai learned about the decree of Haman, he tore his garments and put on sackcloth and ashes. As soon as the royal command reached each province, the Jews living there began mourning and fasting and weeping and wailing, for death was staring them in the face.

When Esther heard about Mordecai's behavior, she sent an attendant to inquire what the matter was. "Give this message to the queen," Mordecai responded. "You must save us from death. No one else can halt this royal decree. It is time for you to go to the king and speak in favor of the Jews of the Persian realm."

When Esther heard these words, she sighed and thought about her uncle's request. "Tell my uncle," she said, laying her hand upon her attendant's arm, "that I have not been summoned into the king's presence for almost one month. Who knows when he shall call for me again? It is against the law to go unbidden into the presence of the king. The last queen lost her diadem when she did not come into the presence when called. Shall I lose the royal favor by entering the royal presence when I have not been called?"

"Then you must go unbidden," came the reply. "I know what it is that I ask, my child, but remember that the life of our entire people rests in your lovely small hands. Do not suppose that because you are in the king's palace, you will be the one Jew to escape. If you remain silent at such a time, God will deliver the Jews by another hand." Mordecai knew how deeply these words would trouble his beautiful niece. "Who knows? Perhaps she has come to the throne for this very calamity," he said to himself after the attendant had departed with his message.

Esther dwelt upon Mordecai's words and sent word to him on the following day: "Assemble all the Jews who are now in Susa. Fast and pray for me. Do not eat or drink day or night for three days. My attendants and I shall keep the same fast. At the end of this time, I shall go to the king in spite of the law. If I die, I die.''

Mordecai and the Jews of Susa carried out Queen Esther's instructions.

On the third day when Esther had finished her prayers, she took off her sackcloth and dressed in one of her finest robes, of pure silk with brilliant blue and green birds appliquéd on the shoulders. She perfumed herself and thought of the plan she had been devising during her time of fasting. With two attendants to carry the train of her dress, she set out for the king's chamber. When the guards opened the door, the king looked up to see why they had entered without his permission. "Who dares disturb the king?" he shouted, his face ablaze with anger.

Esther gripped the arms of her sturdy attendants and forced herself to approach the formidable monarch, who had thrown down his scepter in irritation. "Your lordship, I have come before you to request . . ." Esther faltered and fell backward against her attendants. The king rushed forward to hold her in his arms.

"Request what you will, for you are a lily among brambles. Tell me what you desire. Even if it be half my kingdom, it shall be yours." The king was pleased with himself. "You are the loveliest woman in my empire. Your face, brilliant like the shining stars, sparkles more than all the jewels in the royal treasury."

Esther pressed her cheek against the king's large hands and closed her eyes. "Grant my request. Tomorrow is an important day for me. Let the king come with his prime minister Haman to a banquet I intend to hold for them in the evening, and then I shall ask my favor of the king."

When Haman heard that he had been invited to dine with the queen, he was very excited. Wearing a magnificent gold turban and cloak of fine linen trimmed in purple, symbols of royal favor, he ran all the way home. "Only the king and me," Haman said to himself all the way home from the palace. "Just we three, Esther, the king, and me." He rushed into the courtyard, where his wife Zeresh was sipping spiced wine with some of their relatives.

"I am the second most important man in the kingdom. Once I made the decree to destroy the Jews, and now I have been invited to dine with the queen."

"And I am the second most important woman. My robes are of the same silk as the queen herself wears. My perfumes and oils are kept in gold jars, and my strings of pearls touch my knees." Zeresh stood up and unwound the ropes of pearls from her throat to prove the truth of her statement.

"And the fountains in your courtyard are second only to the fountains of the king," her mother added proudly.

Zeresh handed her husband a silver plate of raisin cakes and figs. "And our ten sons are wise as princes and as clever as their father."

"It is true," said Haman. "I am an important man."

The following evening at the banquet Esther filled the wine goblets and danced to please the king. When Ahasuerus had drunk and eaten his fill, he turned to his queen. "And what is it that your heart desires? Tell me what you want. Even if it be half my kingdom, I shall grant your request."

Haman leaned forward on his couch to hear what it was that the queen might ask of the monarch. Esther lowered her eyes and spoke in hushed tones. "If I have found favor in your eyes, and if it is your pleasure to grant my request, then I ask that you return tomorrow night, you and your minister Haman, to a banquet that I shall hold. And then I shall do as the king asks and make known my request."

Haman ran home, elated by the queen's invitation. "To-morrow night I shall go again to the queen's banquet, and then she will tell the king what she wants. Just we three: Esther, the king, and me!"

"Then indeed you must be the happiest man in the world," one of his sons cried. "All the people in the king-dom bow to our father."

"I would be the most honored man in the kingdom if Mordecai the Jew did not sit in the city gate and refuse to bow when I pass. It is Mordecai who prevents me from being the most important man at the court of King Ahasuerus."

Zeresh folded her arms and spoke sharply to her hus-band. "You complain about Mordecai every night when you pass through our gate. If you are the most important min-ister in the kingdom, then you must order that he be killed. Into the fire you cannot cast him for his ancestor Abraham was saved from it; by the sword you cannot slay him for Isaac his ancestor was saved from it; in water you cannot drown him for Moses, Aaron, and the Israelites were saved from it. Into the lion's den you cannot cast him, for the prophet Daniel was saved from it. Therefore you must erect a stake seventy-five feet high, and tomorrow morning as soon as you have entered the king's chamber, request that he have Mordecai hanged from it."

While Haman lay in his bed that night, imagining his enemy Mordecai finally being silenced, a sneer played across his lips. "Tomorrow will be the most exciting day of my life," he thought, and promptly fell asleep.

At the same time in the palace the king lay awake. He stared at the ceiling and thought about edicts he might issue, he called for musicians to play for him, he sipped a hot drink, but he could not fall asleep. Finally he ordered his attendants to read to him from his favorite book, the

Annals of the Reign of Ahasuerus. "Begin with the entries from two years ago and read up until now. Go no further than what has already happened."

"We have not yet written what has not yet happened," admitted one of the scribes.

"Then you must do so as soon as it happens," the king cried and tossed around in his bed. "Now read to me from the past."

The scribe cleared his throat and read to the king an account of how two of the king's guards had intended to assassinate the king. But Mordecai had uncovered the crime and reported it before the criminals had a chance to set their plot into motion.

"Now read of the great honor and dignity that I conferred upon Mordecai for saving my life," the king said, settling himself among the pillows.

"There was no honor and dignity conferred upon Mordecai. You made Haman the keeper of the king's seal."

The next morning Haman got out of bed full of resolve to follow Zeresh's plan. The stake was erected within sight of the courtyard of his home before he departed for the palace. As soon as he reached the outer room of the king's chamber, the guards called out to him, "The king is anxious to see you immediately. He slept not one wink last night. The royal eyes never closed."

Haman rushed into the king's presence with his request ready on his lips. "Good morning, your lordship, I wish to make a request—"

"The royal eyes did not close last night. I did not sleep a wink. What is the correct way to treat a man whom the king wishes to honor?"

Haman's eyes grew round with surprise. "The king could not wish to honor any person more than the second most important man in his kingdom," he thought. Haman saw himself in the silk robe of deepest purple reserved for the king, riding the king's own stallion, being cheered by the people. Trumpets would play, women would throw flowers in his path. And most definitely Mordecai would bow, his nose to the ground. And then Mordecai would be hanged.

Haman turned to the king. "I think the king would do the greatest honor by allowing the person"—he paused for a moment—"whoever that person might be, to wear the royal robes and ride the royal stallion through the city square—"

"Yes, yes!" The king nodded excitedly. "And then the man shall be led through the streets of Susa while the king's minister proclaims before him, 'This is the way a man shall be treated whom the king wishes to honor.'"

"Excellent, your majesty," Haman looked greedily at the royal robe.

"It shall be done, just as you have described, Haman. Take the purple robes and the horse to Mordecai the Jew, who will be at the city gate, and on no account may you leave out a single detail. You will proclaim my proclamation immediately." And the king left the chamber to return to his bed. After issuing such a momentous proclamation, he felt the royal eyes might finally close.

After the procession, Haman walked slowly away from the palace. He felt as though the eyes of the people of Susa were watching him from behind the shutters of their homes. "'This is the way a man shall be treated whom the king wishes to honor'? How could the king treat his most valued minister in such fashion?" He put the violet edge of his fine linen robe across his face and continued to walk alone through the streets to his house.

Zeresh awaited him at the gate. "When shall Mordecai get what he deserves?" she asked with a wicked smile.

"Mordecai was led around the city square in the king's

robe, riding upon the king's stallion. While the people cheered, I had to lead Mordecai around the square and through the streets.''

"That is not funny. You are in a most peculiar frame of mind, Haman," Zeresh scolded her husband.

"I do not joke. I had to proclaim that the king wished to honor Mordecai, and the people bowed to him." He covered his face in shame. "It did happen, just as I described it. The people of Susa bowed to Mordecai."

"Then as I see it, you are beginning to fall, and Mordecai the Jew to rise. Riding the king's stallion, wearing the king's robes. With him set against you, Haman, your days as keeper of the king's seal are numbered. Mordecai will wear the gold turban and the royal robe of violet and white. And then what will become of your family?"

Two of the king's guards rode up to the gate of Haman's house to escort him to the banquet that Esther was holding. As they rode away, Haman heard Zeresh cry out, "What will become of me?"

When Haman was led into the queen's apartments, the king was seated on a couch piled high with embroidered pillows. Ahasuerus was drinking wine from a new goblet that Esther had had crafted solely for the royal pleasure. It was made of the finest gold with a large handle in the form of a winged lion. Nothing like it had ever before been seen in Susa.

"I shall taste more spiced wine from this most wondrous goblet," said King Ahasuerus to Esther, who immediately served the king. Haman looked on from his couch, drinking ordinary wine from an ordinary goblet. "Tonight I am an ordinary man," he thought to himself.

After Esther had filled the golden goblet several more times, she offered the king a sweetmeat from her hands. He leaned toward his beautiful wife. "And what is it that your heart desires? Tell me what you want. Even if it be half my kingdom, I shall grant your request."

"If I have found favor in your eyes, and if it please your majesty to grant the request of your servant Esther, then grant me my life. That is my request. What I want is the lives of my people. For we have been handed over, my people and I, all of us to be slaughtered. I should not have said anything at all to my lord had we merely been sold as slaves and servants, but with the edict that has been issued by the king's minister, the king will sustain a terrible loss to his kingdom."

King Ahasuerus interrupted Queen Esther. "Who is this man?"

"The enemy of the court. The persecutor of your majesty's friends is none other than Haman."

Haman's goblet fell from his hands. He quaked with terror and stared pleadingly at the monarch. "Oh, your majesty," he whispered, his voice a rasp not heard by the king.

"This wretch shall be ruined," Ahasuerus exclaimed. Full of rage, the king stormed out of the room and paced the garden that surrounded the queen's apartments.

Haman got up from his couch and threw himself at the feet of the queen. "Oh, your majesty, have mercy on this poor man. I have ten sons and a mother-in-law and cousins and relations to support in my household. Think kindly of your servant Haman. It was I who told the king to choose you from all the women of the seraglio. I knew you were the loveliest. . . ." Unable to plead his case any further, Haman buried his head in the pillows at the foot of the queen's couch.

The king returned with several guards to the banquet hall. "What is this?" he shouted, at the sight of Haman, collapsed on the couch where Queen Esther was reclining. "Does this man fall on top of my wife while I am walking about in the garden? Guards! Cover his face!"

The guards seized the miserable Haman and dragged him across the marble floor. Esther looked up at the king. "There is a huge gallows that Haman has prepared for Mordecai, my uncle, who spoke up and saved the life of Ahasuerus, the ruler of the entire Persian realm."

"Yes, yes, let Haman be hanged from the stake he prepared for Mordecai." He smiled at Esther. "And you and Mordecai shall receive all Haman's property and vast wealth."

The next day with Mordecai her uncle at her side, Esther went to visit the king in his chamber. She bowed and kissed the hem of the king's robe. "Haman has been hanged this day. And now if it please the king, and if I have found favor in the king's eyes, could the ten sons of Haman be hanged, as he planned to destroy the Jews, the family of Mordecai?"

"I have given you all Haman's property. And if you wish to destroy his house, write whatever you please regarding Haman and the Jews. Write it in the king's name and seal it with the king's signet. For any edict written in the king's name and sealed with his royal signet is irrevocable."

The royal scribes were summoned and Mordecai dictated an edict to all the Jews and to all the satraps and governors of the one hundred twenty-seven provinces of the Persian empire, to each province in its own script and to each nation in its own language. Copies of the edict were carried by royal messengers riding the fastest horses from the king's own stable. The edict, signed with the king's own seal, proclaimed

> *That King Ahasuerus has found that the Jews, marked*
> *for annihilation by the arch scoundrel Haman, are in*
> *fact governed by the most just of laws. People of the*
> *provinces will therefore do well not to act on the*

edict sent by Haman since their author had been hanged
at the gates of Susa, a fitting punishment for one who
would wish destruction on those innocent of any crime.

That all Jews in whatever city they live have the
right to annihilate any armed force of any people or
province that might attack them together with their
women and children and to plunder their possessions on
the same day throughout the provinces of King
Ahasuerus, and that day shall be the thirteenth day of
the twelfth month, which is Adar.

That day, when Mordecai left the king's presence, he was wearing a royal robe of violet and white, a magnificent gold turban, and a cloak of fine linen trimmed in purple. When the people of Susa saw that he had been rewarded and honored as the second most important man in the Persian empire, they cheered. For the Jews of Susa and throughout every province and in every city, there was great feasting and rejoicing. When the people of the land heard of the edict and that Mordecai had become the king's most cherished counselor, they offered friendship to the Jews, because that was the prudent thing to do.

On the thirteenth day of the twelfth month, which is Adar, when both Haman's command and the king's edict were to be enforced, and the day when the enemies of the Jews had hoped to destroy them, the opposite happened. The Jews gathered in all the cities of the one hundred twenty-seven provinces and destroyed their enemies. They killed all those who had wished to kill them. But most of the governors and satraps and provincial leaders and the people of the land refused to fight the Jews. Instead they appointed Jewish magistrates in order to please Mordecai, who had become the king's cherished adviser.

On the fourteenth day of Adar in the provinces and on

the fifteenth day of Adar in the capital of Susa the Jews celebrated their great victory of deliverance with feasting and sending baskets of sweetmeats to one another. And Mordecai sent official letters to all the Jews, near and far, in all the provinces, that they and their children and their children's children should now and forever keep the fourteenth and fifteenth days of Adar for a celebration and feast to remember for all time the thirteenth of Adar, a day their enemies had marked for Jewish grief and mourning. A day that, because of Queen Esther, became a day of Jewish rejoicing and victory.

Queen Esther, with the full authority of the king, fixed this holiday as Purim, since Haman had cast the *pur* to set the day of destruction, and it was preserved in writing. And Mordecai remained the second most important man in the kingdom of King Ahasuerus all the days of his life. He sought the best interests of the people and was honored by all.

NOTES

The book of Esther tells how the threatened destruction of the Jewish people was averted without the loss of one Jewish life, owing to the courage and wisdom of the Jewish queen, Esther. The story of Esther exists in two versions: the ten-chapter form that appears in the Hebrew Bible and in Protestant translations of it, and the sixteen-chapter form appearing in the Septuagint (Greek) version of the Bible and in Roman Catholic translations. We have followed the Hebrew text, amplifying it with some material from the Greek, such as the text of Mordecai's edict, and with material from the First Targum to Esther.

Although the king of Persia is mentioned 190 times in the Hebrew version of the text, God is never mentioned directly. This may explain why there was much discussion among ancient rabbis about including the book of Esther in the Bible.

The names Esther and Mordecai recall the names of the Babylonian gods Ishtar and Marduk. According to the Targums, Esther's Hebrew name, Hadassah, means "myrtle." Haman is called Haman the Agagite. No place by that name is known, and Agagite probably means a descendant of Agag, the Amalekite king spared by Israel's King Saul in violation of God's command to destroy all the Amalekites (1 Samuel 15). Mordecai is a descendant of Kish, Saul's father, and thus the hostility between the two men reflects the ancient hostility between the Israelites and the Amalekites that goes all the way back to Exodus 17.

In the Hebrew text, the king is called Ahasuerus, which in Persian means simply "the chief of rulers." It is generally agreed that the king meant is Xerxes I, son of the Persian king Darius, who ruled the Persian empire from 485 to 465 B.C.E. Although there are many details that have been confirmed from extrabiblical sources, such as the size of the empire and its impressive postal system and record-keeping habits, the book of Esther is, like the books of Daniel and Judith, a work of fiction seasoned with historical elements. Xerxes' queen was Amestris, who would have belonged to the Persian nobility, and it is highly unlikely that there would have been a Jewish queen on the Persian throne, especially during a time when the Jews were threatened with extinction. Such coincidences—another is that the king's insomnia occurs on the very night Haman is plotting Mordecai's death— add to the story's excitement.

The book of Esther explains the origin of the festival of Purim, or "lots," celebrating the deliverance of the Jews from their enemies. The name comes from the Persian word *pur,* referring to the lot cast by Haman, apparently to determine the best day to carry out his plan to destroy the Jews. Purim remains a major Jewish festival, an occasion for parties, gift giving, and charity. Its principal religious ceremony is the reading of the book of Esther, in the evening and in the morning.

Judith

*M*any years ago in the town of Bethulia there lived a very old woman named Judith. She lived simply and quietly in a large house that had belonged to her husband Manasseh. Every morning and every evening she offered prayers for herself and for all Israel. The people of Bethulia prayed that God might bless them with daughters as beautiful and pious as Judith. She lived alone with her servants, and her young relatives visited her often. They loved to hear the stories of earlier times when Israel's enemies threatened its existence. Very few people in Bethulia were still alive who remembered Judith's husband, for he had died about seventy years earlier when she was very young.

Judith inherited from Manasseh a great estate, flocks and herds, and servants. They had no children, and since she did not wish to become dependent on her nephews, she hired a woman to manage her household.

On warm afternoons young people gathered in the courtyard of Judith's house, near a pool of deep green water, to listen to the old woman's stories.

"Tell us again the story of how you saved our people!" asked one of the girls, her hand trailing in the cool water.

"Yes, tell us about Holofernes and the siege to our own town of Bethulia!"

Judith gathered her robe around her thin shoulders. Even though it was a warm afternoon and she sat in her usual place in the sun, she felt the chill of old bones, as her servant Arba used to say.

"Long ago there was a king named Nebuchadnezzar," she began, "who ruled over the Assyrians in the renowned city of Nineveh, a city so great that it took three days to journey across it."

"And the people of Nineveh did not know their right hand from their left—" one of the girls exclaimed.

"Let Judith continue," another scolded her.

"In those days Arphaxad ruled over the Medes in the city of Ecbatana. He built a great wall around Ecbatana to protect it. It was made out of hewn stones, and was one hundred and five feet high and seventy-five feet thick. The people thought they were safe from all harm behind their massive wall of stone, and they laughed at the threats of the Assyrian king.

"King Nebuchadnezzar went to war against King Arphaxad, calling on all the peoples from Persia to Syria, and from Lebanon all the way to Egypt, even to the borders of Ethiopia, to join him in battle. Our people too he ordered to fight under his generals against the king of Ecbatana. But the leaders ignored his orders, for they were not afraid of

Nebuchadnezzar. This made Nebuchadnezzar furious and he swore by his throne and his kingdom that he would take revenge upon them. So as soon as he had crushed the army of Arphaxad and conquered Ecbatana, looted its bazaars, and turned its splendor to abject ruin, he sent his general, Holofernes, to lay siege to all the cities that had mocked him. And he ordered Holofernes to destroy everyone who refused to kneel to him. 'If the people do not kneel, leave nothing standing.'

"Holofernes was the chief general of the army, second only to Nebuchadnezzar himself, and a man greatly to be feared. Nebuchadnezzar gave him orders to attack the entire West Country, covering the whole face of the earth with the feet of his army.

"Holofernes assembled all his commanders, his generals, and his officers, and mustered troops by divisions, following Nebuchadnezzar's orders. He had one hundred twenty thousand foot soldiers and twelve thousand archers on horseback. They took vast numbers of camels and donkeys and mules for transport, and hundreds upon hundreds of sheep, oxen, and goats for provision, as well as plenty of food for every man, and bulging sacks of gold and silver from the royal treasury. Thus Holofernes set out with his whole army, to go ahead of King Nebuchadnezzar and to cover the whole face of the earth to the west with their chariots and horsemen and select troops of infantry.

"One by one the dreadful Holofernes began to conquer the territories that had mocked Nebuchadnezzar, and the fear and terror of him fell upon people everywhere. As he entered each town, he gathered all the conquered peoples into the town square and warned them, 'If you refuse to obey Nebuchadnezzar, the most powerful ruler in the world, your wounded shall fill every valley; every brook and river shall be dammed up with your dead. Look each of you to the man on his left. For his eye shall not be spared, and his wife shall be taken captive and his children shall be slaves.' "

Judith's voice rang out and the children shivered at the thought of the general's threats.

"Not surprisingly the people of the seacoast surrendered to him; not a single person objected. They welcomed the Assyrian general with garlands and dancing," Judith continued, a smile on her lips. No matter how many times she told the story, the young people's eyes grew wide with wonder as she described those frightening days of war and siege. In their lives they had known only peace and prosperity. Threats of a foreign army were exciting stories to them.

"Holofernes continued to spread fear thick as plague wherever he went. He demolished shrines and sacred places, and demanded that the peoples of the sea, of Sidon and Tyre and Ashkelon, worship only Nebuchadnezzar and call upon him as their god.

"By this time the people of Israel living in Judea heard accounts of the conquests of the Assyrian army. All the cities along the seacoast had fallen, and now the mighty army's breath could be felt on the necks of their own people. Just over the great ridge, Holofernes was camped near the edge of the Esdraelon plain, at Dothan. The people were frightened for the safety of Jerusalem and for the temple of God. Remember, our people had only recently returned from captivity and rebuilt the temple, which had been devastated, leveled to the ground. It was a glorious day when the temple was consecrated and the sacred vessels were sparkling anew and the scrolls were placed inside the ark. And now the sacred altar was in danger of being profaned once again.

"At the order of Joakim, the high priest, and the council of elders of the whole people of Israel, all our people cried out to God and humbled themselves with fasting and prayer. All the men and women and children and every foreigner living among us and hired laborer and slave, even the cattle, girded themselves with sackcloth. And they surrounded the altar with sackcloth and cried out to God not to let the cities they had inherited be destroyed. With ashes upon their turbans, Joakim the high priest and all the priests cried out with all their might for the Lord God to look with favor upon the whole house of Israel.

"Without delay the Israelites seized the passes winding high up into the hills, to prevent Holofernes' army from invading Judah and reaching the temple at Jerusalem. They fortified the villages that stood on the high hilltops and stored up food in case the Assyrian army attacked, since it was soon after the harvest and the fields were bare. When Holofernes received word that the people of Israel had closed the hill passes and set up barricades in the plains, he called together the princes of Moab and the military leaders of Ammon and asked them about the small band of people living in the hills. 'Why have they alone, of all the people who live in the West, refused to come out and honor me?'

"Then Achior, the leader of the Ammonites, stepped forward and bowed to the Assyrian general. 'My lord, I will tell you the truth about this people. By my word not a single falsehood will fly from my lips. The people you ask about are descended from the Chaldeans. They left the ways of their ancestors to worship the God of Heaven; indeed they were driven off by their own people, who worshiped other gods. They fled to Mesopotamia and dwelt there for a long time. Then this God of theirs commanded them to leave Haran and go to the land of Canaan, and the God showed them the way. They prospered with very much cattle, gold, and silver. But a famine spread across the land, and they were forced to go down into Egypt, where there were bulging storehouses of grain, enough for seven years. The people grew in numbers and became such a multitude, like the dust of the earth itself, that the pharaoh became suspicious of them. He forced them to work in the fields and to make bricks. He made slaves of them, and he worked them harder than people had ever been worked, but he could not humble them.

" 'Again their God was with them. The entire land of Egypt was struck with diabolic plagues, frogs, lice, and locusts, and even the great river Nile ran red with blood, they say. The Egyptians pursued them to the sea, and there God split wide the raging sea for the Israelites to cross and folded the sea back upon their enemies, drowning the entire army, horsemen and chariots. And the God of Heaven led them by way of Sinai and Kadesh-barnea through the wilderness.'

"Achior paused and drank from the cup his water-bearer held out to him. Holofernes urged him to continue. 'Is this God with the Israelites even now?'

" 'They dwelt in the land of the Amorites and destroyed all the inhabitants of Heshbon. They crossed the Jordan River in the time of the floods, and once again this God of theirs dried up the water and the people walked across on dry land. As long as they did not sin against their God, they prospered, for the God who hates iniquity is with them. But when they disobeyed the way of their God, they lost every battle, and the temple in Jerusalem was totally destroyed. Not a single stone or pillar was left standing. Their cities were possessed by foreign enemies. But now they have returned to the ways of their God. Where they were once scattered in small numbers in the lands of other peoples, they have returned and even inhabited the hill country, where no one has dwelt. They have rebuilt their temple in Jerusalem—'

" 'And Nebuchadnezzar, the only God in the West, shall raze it to the ground,' vowed Holofernes.

" 'Only if they have sinned against their God shall we prevail,' Achior answered. 'But if they have obeyed their God, then we shall be thrown to the ground before the entire world.'

"The other military men around Achior began to laugh. 'These people of Israel know nothing about waging war. Shall they outflank the mighty Holofernes? Shall Nebuchadnezzar, who rules the whole world, not rule this tiny land also?'

" 'By our swords, let us follow Holofernes, let the vast army of Nebuchadnezzar eat them up,' the commanders shouted.

"With the tip of his sword Holofernes ripped Achior's robe. 'And who are you to prophesy against Nebuchadnezzar, the lord of the whole earth? We will burn up the people in the hills; their mountains will be soaked with their blood. And you, Achior, you shall not see my face again until I have taken my revenge against this people who fled before the Egyptian pharaoh.'

"Holofernes commanded that Achior be bound hand and foot and left lying at the foot of the hill nearest the Israelites' encampment. 'If you have such faith in the God of this people, then you shall be destroyed with them,' the general ordered. Achior lay on the ground, still as a stone, till he was found by an Israelite scouting party and brought back to Bethulia.

"The next day Holofernes ordered his entire army of one hundred and seventy thousand foot soldiers and twelve thousand cavalry to surround Bethulia and seize the important passes up into the hill country. Those passes were so narrow that only two men could squeeze through the rocky walls at a time. When the Israelites saw the horde of Assyrians, thick as a cloud of locusts, below them on the plain, they were terrified. They said, one to another, 'These Assyrian jackals will lick up the face of the whole land; neither the high mountains nor the low valleys can bear their weight.' Israelite soldiers kindled their fires and waited on watch through the long night, in dread of daylight.

"In the morning, as soon as the men had broken camp, Holofernes paraded the entire cavalry before the Israelites of Bethulia. They studied the approaches to the city, and Holofernes posted a guard around the spring that supplied all the water to Bethulia to keep the people from visiting it. 'Thirst will destroy them, and we will not have to throw a single spear.' The commanders congratulated one another on their clever tactic.

"The people of Bethulia gathered in the town square. 'We will die of famine. Nebuchadnezzar will have our bodies as surely as if we had gone to war.'

" 'We must pray to God to strengthen us and deliver us from our enemy,' the elders cried. The people prayed every morning and every evening. And the army of Holofernes stayed by the spring and taunted the thirsting Israelites by pouring pitchers of water on the ground.'"

"You were in Bethulia that day, weren't you, Judith?" One of the young listeners leaned toward the old woman.

"Yes, indeed. I had been a widow for a little more than three years. I lived in this very house and spent most of my days in fasting in a small tent I had set up on the roof. As each day passed and the water level in the cisterns dropped, the people's fears rose. Children began to faint in the street, women and some of the old men fell down panting from thirst. Dust clogged the nostrils, grain could no longer be cooked into cereal. And the people began to speak against the elders. I was angry at such lack of faith, and I urged some of the elders to remind the people of our obligation to be faithful to God."

"They would listen to you because everyone knew of your great devotion to God. My grandmother used to tell me when I was a little girl that a pious woman is to be praised, but a beautiful and pious woman like Judith is more precious than jewels."

Judith shook her head. "Beauty is a toy of the young. It is what is inside the heart that pleases God."

"But you were the most beautiful woman in the whole city," one of the girls exclaimed.

"And now I am the oldest woman in the city," Judith said, laughing. "Well, now, where was I? Oh yes, the elders had promised the people that they would surrender to Holofernes in five more days if God had not come to our aid by then. Imagine that! Testing God! What fools those men were." Judith's voice still trembled in righteous anger seventy years after the elders had agreed to surrender. "The elders could not plumb the depths of the human heart or understand what human beings were thinking. How could they possibly hope to search out God, who made all the wondrous things of the earth and sky?

"When the elders arrived at the house, we sat in this very courtyard, where that grape arbor was heavy with fruit. And I told them that God is not like an enemy, to be threatened, or like a friend, to be won over with pleading. 'Let us call upon our God,' I said, 'all our voices together, and if God chooses to hear us, then God will deliver us. For God is putting us to the test, just as God tested Abraham and Sarah, Isaac and Jacob.'

"I did not wait for them to discuss what they must do. I said, 'I am getting ready to do something that will be remembered through all generations of our descendants. Stand at the city gate tonight, all of you, and with my maid for company, I shall go out of Bethulia. Before the five days have passed, before you can surrender our city to our enemy, the Lord will deliver Israel by my hand.'

"When the elders had left my house, I covered my head with ashes and fell to the ground and prayed to the Lord God of Israel." The girls and boys joined Judith as she recited the now famous words of her prayer:

> *"O God, my God, now hear this widow*
> *for you determined the past*
> *and what is happening now, and what will follow.*
> *What is, what will be, has been by your plan,*
> *what has been, has been by your design.*
>
> *"See the Assyrian hordes, glorying in horse and rider,*
> *trusting in spear and shield, in bow and sling.*
> *They have not recognized the Lord,*
> *the one who bends the spear and twists the shield,*
> *to you alone belongs the title of Lord.*
>
> *"O God, my God, now hear this widow,*
> *give me the strength for what I have in mind.*
> *Strengthen this widow's hand,*
> *strike down slave with master,*
> *break their pride by a woman's hand.*
>
> *"For your strength does not lie in numbers*
> *nor your might in the strength of men,*
> *since you are the God of the humble,*
> *the support of the weak, the refuge of the despairing.*
> *O God, hear my prayer."*

"After a while I got up and summoned my servant Arba to help me dress. I removed my sackcloth and my dull widow's garments. I washed myself and covered my body with rich perfume. Arba arranged my hair and wove a band of pearls through the thick braid. I slipped sandals on my feet, and for the first time since the death of my dear husband Manasseh, I wore robes of fine silk and rings of topaz and carnelian and anklets and strings of jewels. From my wrists dangled emerald bracelets and beads.

"I filled a food sack with roasted grain, dried fig cakes, cheese, and bread, and handed it to Arba. For she would accompany me on my journey and aid me in my plan. As we had arranged, the elders opened the city gate and Arba and I made our way down the mountainside, straight into the valley where the army of Holofernes was encamped. We had not gone many steps before we were stopped by an Assyrian patrol.

" 'Whose side are you on? Where do you come from and where are you going?' one of them demanded.

" 'I am Judith, a Hebrew woman. I am fleeing from my people since you will soon overrun their camp and make them your captives. I am on my way to see the great general Holofernes because I wish to show him the road to take through the secret mountain passes so that he may overtake the garrisons on the top of the mountains.'

" 'Your action will be the saving of you,' declared one of the guards.

" 'If the other Hebrew women are as beautiful as you, capturing this people will be a pleasure!'

" 'A delight to possess such exquisite delicate charms,' another one agreed.

" 'Tell our general what you have told us, and he will treat you well.'

" 'When he sees your beauty, and hears your words, you will not regret your decision to come to him.'

"The guards led Arba and me to the general's tent. By the time we got there, we had an escort of about one hundred soldiers, curious to see this Hebrew woman glittering in fine clothes. I must have been a sight, finest silks as though on the way to a royal feast, carrying a sack filled with simple food, followed by a servant in rough linen.

"Holofernes was lying on his bed, under a canopy woven

of purple and gold, studded with emerald and precious stones. His shield, helmet, and armor lay nearby, his double-edged sword hung on the wall over his head. When he saw me, he rose quickly and greeted me politely. I knelt before him and paid him homage. His servant raised me up, and Holofernes had torches brought close so that he might examine my face.

" 'Please listen to what your servant has to say, O great and mighty general. I shall speak no word of falsehood to my Lord tonight.' "

One of the boys clapped his hands. "You meant our Lord God of Israel, and you could not speak falsely to God."

Judith smiled. "I wound my way through the paths of words as though I were leading the general through the mountain passes outside Bethulia. I explained that the people in our town were weak from hunger and were going to consume what God had forbidden them to eat. I could not remain in a town that would sin before God. So I had come to him, before the Lord God destroyed the home of my dead husband and my ancestors.

"I leaned toward Holofernes and spoke from the heart. 'God has sent me to do things with you at which the world will be astonished when it hears.'

"Holofernes touched my cheek. 'God has done well to send you ahead of the others. Strength will be ours, death to those who have insulted my lord Nebuchadnezzar.' He ordered that a table be set with the finest silver, and he invited me to taste the special delicacies that had been prepared for him. But I took some parched grain and dried figs from the food sack I still carried. 'I will not share in the sumptuous provisions of my lord's table in case I should displease my Lord,' I said, and sat at his feet. He drank wine and I ate from my food sack. 'Will your provisions not be gone too quickly?' he asked, his tongue loosening from great gulps from the chalice.

" 'The Lord will have used me to accomplish a great plan before your servant has finished these provisions.'

"He had a tent pitched for me alongside his own, and gave permission for me to leave the camp with my servant Arba to pray before the morning light. For three days I remained in Holofernes' camp, amusing him each evening and then departing the camp to pray and bathe at the spring.

"On the fourth day Holofernes gave a splendid banquet and invited all his servants. It was to be a night of great revelry before we set out for the mountain passes on the following morning. I knew that Holofernes intended to have me in his bed that night, for I had overheard his commanders laughing about his plans outside my tent, but I pretended that I anticipated the evening with great delight. 'I believe that this evening will be one I remember with the deepest joy all the days of my life,' I assured the general's messengers.

"I dressed with great care, and Arba dressed my hair with jewels as she had done four nights earlier. We discussed our plan carefully, and I told her to wait for me that night outside his tent.

"When I was brought in to the presence of Holofernes, I could see desire in his eyes. I sat at his feet and sang a song to him. His hands played in my hair, and I poured wine into his chalice after every time it touched his lips. I think he drank more that night than he ever had in his entire life. And he was no stranger to wine!

"As the evening drew on, Holofernes' attendants withdrew from the tent to go to bed, and the tent was closed from outside. Now I was alone with him in the tent! But he had consumed so much wine that he lay stretched out on his bed, dead drunk. I stood at the side of his bed and looked down at him. How contorted his face was, and how cruel he looked even in a drunken stupor! I said a prayer under my breath, asking God to look upon the work of my hands for the glory of Jerusalem, and to help me destroy our enemies.

"At the end of his bed above his head was his long gleaming sword. My hand closed around its cold metal hilt. With my other hand I grasped the hair of the top of his head. I took a deep breath and brought the blade of the scimitar down with all my might. I raised my arm again, and a second time brought the sword down with all my might and severed his head. Blood spattered my silk robe and over the canopy that hung from the bedposts. Warm blood oozed between my toes."

One of the younger boys hid his face in his sister's lap. Judith patted his shoulder. "Yes, it was a terrible night. My mind can still see clearly every single detail. The body of Holofernes twitched and I jumped back in fright. As soon as the body was still, I rolled it off the bed. Now the proud and haughty general at whose feet I had so often bowed lay prostrate at my feet. Then I pulled down the canopy from the bedpost, and wrapped his bloody head in the purple and gold netting. I paused for a moment at the door and wiped the sweat from the palms of my hands. Very calmly I left the tent and handed the gory wrapping to Arba, who dropped it into our food sack. Then the two of us walked slowly through the sleeping camp as if we were going out to pray. The guards took no notice, as it had been our habit to leave the camp each night.

"We circled round the valley and climbed up the steep slope. The sack seemed to grow heavier as we made our way to the gates of Bethulia. Finally as we approached the gate, I cried at the top of my lungs, 'Open, open the gate! The Lord our God is still with us. God has shown great power over our enemies this day.'

"When the people in the city heard my shouts, men, women, and small children rushed out of their houses and ran to the city gate. They ignited a huge fire for light and gathered around Arba and me. I pulled the head out of the sack and showed it to them in the flickers of the flame. The hair was matted with dried blood. 'Here is the head of Holofernes, commander of the Assyrian army. And here is the canopy under which he lay drunk. The Lord struck him down by the hand of a woman.'

"All the people cheered and pressed close to me. 'May you be blessed by God above all women on earth,' they cried. 'God grant that you will always be held in honor and rewarded with blessings for what you have done.'

" 'Now I know that your God is God, both in heaven above and on earth beneath!' exclaimed Achior, who had remained with our people all this time, praying and entreating God for help.

" 'The Lord our God, creator of heaven and earth, guided you to cut off the head of our enemy,' the elders chimed in.

" 'He was taken in by my beauty, and I tricked him with the cleverness of my plan because it pleased the Lord God of Israel.'

"I told them to take Holofernes' head and hang it at dawn on the wall of the city so that the Assyrians might recognize it, and their hearts melt within them. Our leaders were so excited that they could not attend to the important battle ahead. So I ordered the soldiers to assemble as soon as it was light, and to behave as if they were going to march down to the plain where the Assyrians were camped. But I warned them that they must not attack. For the Assyrians would be seized with panic when they discovered the head of their army was no longer with them. Then it would be easy for the Israelite army to triumph."

"I know what happened next." The youngest of the girls jumped up from her seat and ran to Judith. "The Assyrians saw our army massing on the plain. Their generals ordered their commanders and their commanders ordered the other officers who went to the tent of their general to ask why Holofernes was not prepared to ride out at their head." She giggled at her own cleverness and sat down.

"That is right," said Judith. "Then the servant of Holofernes called out to his leader. When he got no response, he entered the tent of Holofernes and discovered him thrown down dead on the floor with his head lopped off. Then he rushed into my tent, and finding it deserted, he dashed out amid all the soldiers and shouted, 'One Hebrew woman has brought destruction on the whole house of Nebuchadnezzar. Holofernes is lying dead on the floor of his tent, and his head is gone!'

"As soon as the soldiers heard these words, they ran around ripping their garments and shouting in grief and panic. Filled with fear and trembling, they fled through every footpath up through the mountains and down through the valleys. Then all the inhabitants of Bethulia fell on the Assyrian encampment and looted it. I was presented with the drinking bowls and furniture and silver plate and other belongings of the Assyrian general as well as the very tent of Holofernes."

"Do you still have it? Can we see it?" the young people clamored.

Judith laughed. "No, I dedicated all the spoils to the temple in Jerusalem. What a day that was! I took branches of vine leaves and distributed them to the women who were with me, and I and all the women of Bethulia put olive wreaths of victory upon our heads and led the men in singing and dancing. For three months we remained rejoicing in front of the temple at Jerusalem, and I stayed with the people. When we returned to Bethulia, I came back here to my house, where I have stayed ever since in prayer and fasting and thanksgiving for the opportunity God gave me to save our people and to bring peace and prosperity to our land."

"And the Assyrians never bothered us again," one of the young people said. "We will always be safe from harm."

A shadow of sadness crossed Judith's face. "There will always be enemies at our gates. But so long as we obey God's laws, we will prevail."

Judith motioned to some of the older children, "Go into my house and bring out the old leather trunk with scarred straps." They knew what trunk she meant, for it had stood there as long as any of them could remember.

"I am very old and soon I will be gathered to my people. I have set all my servants free and given them money to begin new lives. And now it will be my pleasure to give you my jewelry and silver and silk robes and goblets and chalices." As she spoke, Judith handed around all the items in her trunk.

As the young people bade her good-bye, they understood the gravity of the occasion. And they wondered if they would ever see Judith again.

N O T E S

The book of Judith may have originally been written in Hebrew but is transmitted to us in Greek translation. Whereas the book is highly regarded by both Jews and Christians, Jews and Protestants do not include it in their Bibles, while Roman Catholics do. Although Judith is written as though it were a history, it abounds with historical inaccuracies. The book is now considered by many scholars to be a work of fiction in which the author has freely knitted together various scraps and moments of history. Its historical setting adds to the flavor of the story, like the historical romances people read today.

The name Judith in Hebrew is the feminine form of "Jew," or

a person from Judea, and indicates the mythic quality of Judith's story. It is likely that the story was written during the time of the Maccabean struggles, when the real enemy of the Jewish people was not Nebuchadnezzar as the story tells us, but the Seleucid ruler Antiochus IV, Epiphanes, who in 168 B.C.E. desecrated the temple in Jerusalem. Judith's life-span, one hundred and five years, may represent the period of Jewish rule over Judea under the Hasmoneans.

The irony that abounds in the story has delighted audiences through the centuries. A widow, one of the traditionally weakest members of ancient Israelite society, has the courage and wit that is lacking in the male elders of the city; and with her superior tactics, she is able to defeat the powerful Assyrian army. Judith's smooth speeches when she addresses Holofernes are full of double meanings, as for example, when she says, "God has sent me to do things with you at which the world will be astonished when it hears." When she refers to "my Lord" having success, she means the God of Israel, but the arrogant Holofernes thinks she is speaking of him.

As in the story of David and Goliath, the "weak" hero Judith triumphs over the strong enemy and cuts off his head, overcoming seemingly impossible odds with divine assistance. Judith is reminiscent of a number of other famous women in the Bible. She leads her people in song and dance like the prophet Miriam, she kills an enemy violently like Jael, she gives military advice like Deborah, and her beauty, like that of Sarah, is unsurpassed. The theme of the book resembles closely that of Esther.

A Mosaic for Miriam

*O*ften women are mentioned fleetingly in biblical narra-
tives. They are only bits or pieces of someone else's story.
The names of many of them have been lost, and we know
them only as someone's daughter, or someone's wife, or
someone's mother. Since they do not get to tell their own
stories in the Bible, we have given them that opportunity
here in our book, in the hope that readers will remember
them after they have listened to the women's own "voices."

Job's Wife

My husband Job and I lived in the land of Uz with our seven sons and three daughters. Life was very good. We had plenty of herds of sheep and goats. I had gold rings for every finger and strings of gold beads and fine brooches set with every precious stone. Job used to recite to himself with pleasure the size of his holdings, "I own seven thousand sheep, three thousand camels, five hundred yoke of oxen, and five hundred donkeys, and many many servants besides!" Everyone agreed my husband Job was the most prosperous of all the Edomites. God had blessed our lives.

One day when our sons and daughters were eating and drinking at their oldest brother's house, a messenger came to Job. "Your oxen were at the plow, and the donkeys grazing at their side, when the Sabeans swept down on them and carried them off and put the servants to the sword. I alone escaped and rushed to tell you the bad news."

That was the beginning of the stream of news that would turn anyone silent with shock. But not my husband Job. "At least my children are safe," he said and blessed God.

Another messenger hurried in to tell him that the Chaldeans had raided and stampeded the camels and killed more of the servants. The man trembled as he related his story. "I alone escaped and rushed to tell you the bad news."

"At least my family is safe," Job repeated and blessed God.

A third messenger came to the house that night and told Job, "While your seven sons and three daughters were eating and drinking in celebration today, a great fierce wind sprang up from the desert and it battered the four walls of the house, which fell in on the young people. They all were crushed. I alone escaped and rushed to tell you the bad news."

Surprisingly Job took that dreadful news equally well. I held my tongue and grieved quietly for my dead daughters and sons. My husband Job has always enjoyed suffering and this was the greatest suffering he had ever endured.

Prostrating himself Job cried out,

> *"Naked I came forth into this world,*
> *And naked I shall return to it.*
> *The Lord gave, the Lord has taken away,*
> *Blessed be the name of the Lord."*

Naturally the bad news spread fast throughout the town of Uz and far beyond. Job's three best friends, Eliphaz, Bildad, and Zophar, hurried to bring him consolation and sympathy. They wept aloud and tore their clothes and threw dust over their heads, behaving like proper mourners. They sat on the ground beside my husband Job for seven days and seven nights. They never said a word to Job, and he never said a word to them. Everyone respected Job because his suffering was so great.

After his seven days of silence, Job began to suffer loudly. "I am blameless. How can God treat me as though I were perverse? I am innocent, but I loathe my life!"

I listened to my husband for as long as I could. Finally I said to him, "If you are so certain that you are blameless, then curse God, and die. Death will put an end to all your pain and suffering."

Job was surprised by my suggestion, then angry. "How can you be such a foolish woman? Shall we accept good at the hand of God, and shall we not expect to receive evil?"

"You are the one covered with boils. You are the one demanding comfort." I did not speak to my husband directly again. But I watched as he argued with his friends about what God might do and might not do. I listened as he insisted upon his innocence, and his three comforters assured him that if he was really so innocent, God would not have allowed such misery to befall him.

"Maybe your children sinned. Although you claim no guilt, maybe wickedness has dwelt in your tents." Eliphaz sat next to Job on the ground.

"Perhaps you forgot to pray. The hope of the godless man shall perish; he leans against his house, but it does not stand," Bildad chimed in.

"You say that you are pure in God's eyes, but can you find out the deep things of God?" Zophar asked.

For days the arguments continued. At first it seemed as though Job were on trial, and later as though the very Lord God were on trial.

Finally Job cried out to God, "I have uttered what I did not understand, things too wondrous for me, which I did not know. I had talked about you with my tongue and I had heard about you with my ears; but now I understand with my heart and mind, and nothing looks the same to me as before."

Job prayed for his friends and for himself, and God accepted Job's prayer and blessed Job. Now Job, a man from the land of Uz, had fourteen thousand sheep, six thousand camels, a thousand yoke of oxen, and a thousand donkeys. Once again Job had seven sons and three daughters. The daughters, Turtledove, Cassia, and Mascara, were the most beautiful in the land of Uz. They were also very wealthy, for their father gave them each a generous inheritance. If my father had given me an inheritance, I would not have stayed silent all those years, depending on my husband, Job, to support me!

As you see, everything that had been taken from him was restored to Job. Except for me. Rumors spread throughout Uz that I had run off with an adversary of my husband.

Huldah the Prophet

In the eighteenth year of the reign of King Josiah, a great building project was in process. The king had proclaimed that the Temple be repaired, and carpenters, masons, and stonecutters were brought from all parts of Judah to work on the restoration. "We shall require no accounting of funds, for everyone working on God's house will deal honestly with us," the king told the keeper of his treasury.

One day Hilkiah, the high priest, said to his secretary, "Workmen have brought this scroll to me. It was found in the house of the Lord and I believe it contains the words of God."

With great care the two men carried the scroll to the king and read aloud to him from its contents. The king was shaken by the words that he heard. "For I shall set before you blessings and curses, the blessing if you obey the commandments of the Lord God, and the curse if you do not obey, but turn aside from the way which I the Lord your God command you, if you go after other gods which you have not known, as you know me."

King Josiah tore at his robes and cried out, "Go, inquire of the Lord. If these words are the true covenant that generations have recited before the Lord God, the wrath of God will surely be kindled against us for not keeping this covenant, for worshiping other gods, for ignoring God's commandments."

"We shall take the scroll to Huldah, the prophet, who lives in Jerusalem," Hilkiah said. "She will discern God's will concerning the teachings set forth in this book. She will know if it is the covenant our ancestors made with the Lord at Sinai."

Huldah took the scroll from the men and unrolled it in her chamber. "I will need to examine these words. I will need time to inquire of the Lord. Return to me in a day's time." The men left her deep in thought, murmuring words from the book.

Throughout the night Huldah studied the scroll and meditated upon its words. When the men returned, she told them that the words of the book were indeed the words of God and must be heeded. "Go and warn the king that God will surely bring evil upon Jerusalem if the teachings of the Book of the Covenant are ignored."

The men took the holy scroll so that it might be returned to the Temple. Huldah accompanied them. "Tell the king that because his heart was penitent, God will deal mercifully with him."

When King Josiah heard the words of Huldah the prophet, he vowed to follow all the teachings and to keep all the commandments and statutes of God. He gathered the people of Jerusalem so that they might hear the words of the Lord. "Hear, O Israel," he read from the scroll, "hear and remember the words of our Lord. We shall have no other God, we shall worship God only at the sanctuary in Jerusalem. We shall destroy all the other places where people go to worship God and present offerings.

"God has promised us this land flowing with milk and honey for all times. But only if we love the Lord with all our hearts, and minds, and strength. And we must teach these words to our children and to our children's children."

And the people listened, and during the lifetime of King Josiah they obeyed the commandments.

Queen Jezebel

A Phoenician princess, Jezebel, was given in marriage by her father Ethbaal to King Ahab of Israel to seal an alliance between their two countries. When she arrived at the palace at Samaria, Jezebel had only her attendants and the prophets of her gods, Baal and Asherah, to accompany her.

Longing for a view of the sea, she stared out her window at the rolling hills of this strange land whose culture was so different from her own. She filled the palace rooms with inlaid ivory carvings from her homeland; she ate fruit from the metal bowl with the embossed lotus medallion that had graced her mother's table when she was a child. Jezebel ordered her attendants to get the special shells that when crushed yielded purple dye that Phoenician women favored. Such a process to make cloth was unknown to the Israelite women living in the hill country. Staring out the window at the road leading up to the entrance of the palace, Jezebel wondered if she would ever truly be queen of this country. She called for the prophets of Baal to console her, and then sent them away again. Could nothing stop Jezebel's longing for her own country?

Because her father had insisted she be taught to read and write together with the princes of the palace, Jezebel was restless in Israel. Her husband preferred holding feasts to holding discussions. To fill her time, she studied books of the laws of her husband's land; she read of their God and taught her husband about her own god Baal. She spoke of the powers of Baal with her prophets and invited them to visit the palace and partake of the king's food. Gradually King Ahab began to appreciate the powers of Baal and ordered that vineyards and forests be planted to honor Baal at Carmel. The people of Israel erected altars to Baal and Asherah. Queen Jezebel felt more at home.

There was one prophet of Israel's God who spoke out against Baal and warned the Israelites against worshiping this false god. His words angered Jezebel mightily. A braggart and a disheveled little man, Elijah by name, he disappeared from sight for several years, during which time Jezebel's prophets became powerful throughout Israel. The king provided for all their needs, and they advised him on important matters of state. The land of Israel suffered from a terrible drought. All the prayers and incantations of the prophets of Baal failed to bring rain and relief to the land. As suddenly as he had dropped out of sight, Elijah reappeared and challenged Jezebel's prophets to a contest on Mount Carmel.

"Go after that loud-mouthed prophet of God and silence him once and for all," cried Jezebel to King Ahab. "He has insulted me and my god for the last time." Jezebel went to the window and watched her husband depart.

King Ahab ordered his chariot to the top of Mount Carmel, where Elijah called upon God. To the shame of the prophets of Baal, Elijah's prayers brought earth-trembling thunder and sky-splitting lightning. And through the will of the Lord God, rain washed away the drought. Filled with triumph and the respect of the Israelites who had witnessed the defeat of the prophets of Baal, Elijah, the prophet of God, slaughtered the four hundred prophets of Baal.

When word of the happenings on Mount Carmel reached Jezebel, she ran through the palace cursing Elijah. "By my god Baal, Elijah's life will be worth no more than the life of one of my dead prophets by this time tomorrow," Jezebel vowed.

To please his wife King Ahab sent messengers after Elijah, to bring him to the palace, but they did not find the prophet. Ahab secretly rejoiced, for the contest on Mount Carmel had proved to him that the Lord God was indeed the true God and that his wife's Baal therefore was a lesser god. But knowing of his wife's devotion to her god, he kept silent. To appease her he sent to Phoenicia for more prophets to dwell at the palace at Samaria. In time Jezebel went back to studying her books and debating with the scribes of Israel and seemed to forget that day of thunder on Mount Carmel.

King Ahab wanted the vineyard in Jezreel that belonged to Naboth. He thought its fertile land would please Queen Jezebel so he sent to Naboth with an offer to buy the vineyard from him. Naboth refused, so the king offered to exchange it for a better vineyard. For a second time, Naboth refused. "God forbid that I should give you my ancestral heritage," he told the king.

King Ahab was very angry. He went to bed and refused to eat. He wouldn't open his eyes unless the queen was in the room. "What is making you so unhappy?" she demanded on the third day.

"Naboth won't trade his vineyard, even if I give him good land for it."

"Some fine king you are! Get out of that bed and eat your dinner. I myself shall get you the vineyard from Naboth. Before the sun shines on his fine vineyard another day, I shall have devised a plan."

Using the king's name and seal, Jezebel wrote letters to the elders of Jezreel, Naboth's city, demanding that they proclaim a fast and be certain that Naboth was given a place of importance among the people. They were to arrange for two wicked men to accuse Naboth of cursing God and King Ahab. "Then take the wretch outside and stone him to death."

The elders followed the instructions in the letters. Two men were found to accuse Naboth. "Naboth has cursed God and the king," they cried out from the middle of the crowd. According to Israelite law, Naboth was pronounced guilty, immediately taken outside the city gates, and stoned to death.

When Jezebel heard the news, she went to her husband's chamber. He was still lying in his bed complaining about the vineyard that he so desperately wanted. "Get up!" she cried. "The vineyard is yours."

Ahab was so delighted that he arranged for a trip to the vineyard to oversee the first planting himself. He was met there by Elijah the prophet of God. "You are a murderous dog," he shouted at the king. "By the word of the Lord God of Israel, as the dogs licked the blood of Naboth in Jezreel, so shall dogs lick your blood too."

"You dare to speak so to the king!" demanded Ahab, but his eyes looked frightened. What if Elijah was right and

God was preparing to bring disaster upon his house?

"You dare to double-deal the Lord God and the people of Israel! You dare displease God in order to please Jezebel!"

When Ahab heard these words, he hurried home and tore his clothes and put on sackcloth and got into bed. He fasted, he slept in the sackcloth, and he cried out to the Lord God of Israel. He could not be comforted, not even by his wife Queen Jezebel.

Many prophets were attracted to the palace at Samaria. They were well treated since their talk amused Jezebel, and many returned often, having acquired a taste for power. False prophets were among them, although their words were impossible to detect from the true. "If you march on Ramoth in Gilead, victory will surely be yours," they advised King Ahab.

The battle was fierce that day, and the Syrians beat back the Israelites. King Ahab's body was returned to Samaria in a chariot stained with blood. His servants washed the chariot by the pool of Samaria and the dogs licked up his blood, according to the word of God that Elijah had spoken.

During the next fourteen years Jezebel remained in the palace and guided the hands of her sons Ahaziah and Jehoram, who ruled over Israel. Like their mother, they worshiped Baal, but they also worshiped the God of Israel, and they encouraged the people to do the same. The God of Israel was aroused by the perfidy of the people of Israel and his prophet Elisha warned of the danger to Israel if they continued to anger God.

Jehu, a commander of the army inspired by God's prophet Elisha, assassinated Jehoram in Jezreel and vowed to eradicate worship of Baal in Israel.

Full of the triumph of killing in the name of the Lord, Jehu set out for the palace to put an end to the Phoenician queen and her worship of Baal.

When Jezebel heard the stirrings in the city, she went

into her chamber and sat down at the table where she kept her cosmetics and ointments. She looked at her reflection in the ivory-handled mirror her daughter Athaliah had given her. Taking a small alabaster jar of kohl, she deftly painted her eyes. She smoothed her hair and adorned her head with jewels. Then she went to the window that overlooked the entrance to the palace. Jezebel was standing there as Jehu entered the gate followed by his soldiers.

"You traitor, murderer of your king, are you indeed looking for peace?" she called, her eyes cold with contempt.

Jehu lifted up his face and looked up at the queen framed in the window. "Who is on my side?" he shouted.

Three of the queen's attendants appeared behind her. Jehu called out to them, "Throw her down."

Rizpah

During his reign over Israel Saul had broken a treaty with the Gibeonites and slaughtered many of them. God had withheld the rain and allowed the scorched earth to deliver withered crops and dried-out grain. In the days of King David, famine ravaged the land for three desperate years.

Each season the fields yielded fewer crops. The earth was parched from lack of rain, and the streams were drying up. To end the famine in Israel, David handed over Saul's descendants to the Gibeonites to satisfy their claim against the royal house. Would these seven deaths be sufficient to cause the rain to fall? Would God allow fat grain to swell in the fields of the land?

King Saul's five grandsons and the two sons Rizpah had borne to King Saul had been exposed on the mountainside, an ignominious end for a royal house of Israel. "Now the famine will end," the people cried. The bodies were left exposed on the mountainside to satisfy the Gibeonites, but still the rain did not fall.

When Rizpah learned that the bodies had not been given a proper burial, she had taken up her place upon a nearby rock, which she covered with sackcloth as a sign of mourning and respect for the dead. Through the heat of the day and the chill of the night, she held her vigil, chasing away birds of prey and wild animals that approached the bodies.

Day after day Rizpah, the daughter of Aiah, sat upon her solitary rock, keeping watch. For six months she had sat, alone, since the beginning of the meager barley harvest. Throughout the long dry summer she alone watched. Now it was time for the autumn rains, but no drop of rain had fallen. Rizpah stared at the cruel, cloudless sky. Such a beautiful bright blue color to bring such pain to the Israelites, who prayed every day for rain. Haggard and exhausted from lack of sleep, Rizpah no longer shed tears. As she continued her lone vigil, she thought of the misery that had befallen the house of Saul.

Saul's son Jonathan had been killed with his father on Mount Gilboa while fighting the Philistines. Saul's daughter Michal had no children, and though her sister Merab had borne five sons, now they, along with Rizpah's sons, lay dead, victims of men thirsting for revenge.

Day after day Rizpah sat upon her solitary rock, keeping watch over the bodies of men.

If only the Gibeonites had asked for silver or gold! Surely King David would have paid them whatever they wanted from the royal coffers! What threat were her young sons to the throne of the mighty David?

"Killing and more killing," thought Rizpah, "shedding the blood of the innocent along with the guilty. Will the sword devour forever? Why can't men see that the end will be bitter?"

Rizpah thought she felt a raindrop on her parched cheek. She raised her fingers to her face. For the first time in months a few wisps of clouds brushed across the sky. The woman was startled by the gentle touch of a hand on her shoulder. A man stood at her side. She looked up at him with dark hollow eyes, but she did not question him.

"Forgive me for disturbing you," he said, "for I can see your anguish. I have been sent to tell you that King David knows of your heroic vigil. He is in your debt for showing honor and respect to the dead. Thus he has commanded that the bones of your sons and the grandsons of King Saul be given a proper burial. Everyone in Jerusalem praises your courage and faithfulness."

The man gently turned Rizpah's shoulders so she could see the soldiers advancing toward them. Under the thin fabric of her robe, he could feel her bones, like the bleached pale bones of the dead lying in front of her. For a moment he was too moved by her wraithlike appearance to speak. "This day the king has ordered a public burial to honor the dead of the house of Saul." Rizpah's eyes met the messenger's for a moment and then she returned her gaze to the horizon. The rain began to fall steadily.

Delilah

When I was a child, I used to dream of becoming a hero, like Jael or like Deborah. Perhaps you have heard the story of Jael, who killed the Canaanite general Sisera, and brought a great victory to Israel in the time of Deborah. She was greatly praised throughout Israel for her valorous deed. "Most blessed of women be Jael, of tent-dwelling women most blessed," they honored her in their victory song. I have heard the song many times. The Israelites who lived among us were fond of singing it, as if they hoped we Philistines would suffer the same fate as the Canaanites under Sisera. "Delilah," my mother would say, "your dreams of heroism are silly daydreams. Besides, we Philistines have many champions, brilliant statesmen, and mighty warriors. We have no need of a woman's cunning to bring us success."

As I grew up, I forgot my childhood dream and never guessed that I would help my people capture an enemy: Samson! I had heard his name many times before I met him. He played wicked pranks and caused trouble for some of our people. Samson! He had burned our fields, overcome our bravest soldiers with only a donkey's jawbone for a weapon, and torn our city gates out of their place—but each time, I confess, our people had provoked him.

He was a handsome man with legs thick as columns and arms

that could hold me helpless at his side as easily as if I were a piece of cloth. I delighted in his words of love and laughed at his riddles and stories. I never tired of hearing about his strength, like the time he killed a lion with his bare hands. We spent many pleasant hours in the grape arbor beside my house. That man could drink wine!

Then one day, in late spring, the lords of the five Philistine cities came to my house in the Valley of Sorek. They came in their chariots, from Ashkelon, Ekron, Ashdod, Gaza, and Gath, dressed in their finest robes, followed by fawning attendants.

"To what do I owe such a great honor, my lords?" I asked as I bowed. "Please, come inside and rest. Allow me to offer you food and drink, for you must be hungry and thirsty after your journey." Could they tell how nervous I was?

"We have no time for food or drink," the ruler of Ashkelon snapped. "We have come to discuss an important matter."

His rudeness helped me find my sharp tongue. "What important matter could the five lords of the Philistines discuss with me? Do you lack counsel regarding affairs of state?"

"Our visit does concern affairs of state, Delilah." The lord of Gaza was more courteous. "We need your help. For years that Israelite strongman Samson has been ravaging our country and intimidating our soldiers. Each time we devise a scheme to capture him, he outwits us."

The ruler of Gath smiled falsely. "Since you have a strong friendship with Samson, we have come to ask you to find out the secret of his strength, so that at last we can make him our prisoner." His smile turned to one of eager anticipation.

"We'll give you eleven hundred pieces of silver if you will help us," added the lord of Gaza.

"Eleven hundred pieces of silver, my lord? Do you think I can be bought? Besides, what is eleven hundred pieces of silver to the rulers of the five Philistine cities, with all their wealth? You obviously don't want the Israelite Samson very badly."

"Each one of us will give you eleven hundred pieces of silver," four of the rulers spoke in unison. The ruler of Gath scowled at them, but nodded his head.

"That is truly a great deal of money, my lords." My eyes took in all the detail of their finely embroidered robes. "But still, it is no easy thing that you ask. Samson is not merely strong, he is also clever." I hesitated for a moment. "And he amuses me." I would not disclose to their greedy eyes how much I cared for Samson.

"But you owe it to your country, Delilah." The ruler of Ashkelon placed a jeweled hand on my shoulder. "Think of all the trouble he has caused our people."

"Think how grateful our people will be. Your praises will be sung throughout the countryside! Your name will be remembered forever!"

I thought of my childhood dreams. I was proud to be a Philistine. We had magnificent cities while the Israelites dwelt in primitive settlements. They were uncouth and uncultured, like Samson, who for all his wit was stronger than he was smart. Perhaps I liked that about him. Still, he wasn't one of us. And he had played cruel tricks on our people. "All right, my lords, I agree. I shall uncover the secret of Samson's great strength, and what you must do in order to capture him. I'll send word to you as soon as I know how we can destroy our enemy."

After the rulers had gone, I imagined the people shouting, "Delilah, you have given our enemy Samson into our hands; may you be praised throughout Philistia!"

"I'll ask him outright," I said to myself, "I'll make no

pretense about it. I'll ask him what makes his strength so great and how a person might capture him."

And so I did. Three times I asked him and three times he made up a story. First he told me he could be captured if I bound him with seven supple bowstrings not yet dried out. Then he told me I should try new ropes that had never been used. The third time he suggested I weave his long, heavy hair together with the flax on my loom. Each time he broke away from my trap, as though I had bound him with paper chains. On the third day, when he yanked his hair from my loom, he moved with such force that he nearly ruined my loom!

But I am persistent. I kept pestering him with questions until finally he told me the true secret of his strength. I could tell from the tremor in his voice and the serious expression on his face that this time there was no trickery, no games in his story.

Samson explained that he was dedicated to his God, and his long hair was a sign of that dedication. If his hair were cut, his God would leave him and his strength would be gone. While Samson slept I summoned the Philistine lords. They brought with them the sacks of silver they had promised. I raised my razor and sheared the wavy locks of my dear Samson. The Philistine rulers bore away their prisoner in triumph. My last view of Samson was of a blinded and defenseless man.

There was a stupendous celebration in Gaza, in honor of our victory over Samson. I expected my people to recognize my sacrifice, but the Philistine lords took all the credit. They boasted that Dagon our god granted them success. Throughout the city the people cried, "Our god has given Samson, our enemy, into our hand." But nowhere did they say, "Most blessed of women be Delilah, of Philistine women most blessed."

I was too discouraged to go to the temple of Dagon to

watch Samson be humiliated before the crowd. Thousands of people were there. When I heard that Samson had pulled down the temple of Dagon, killing all the spectators, I knew that his strength had returned. In spite of all our plans and schemes against him, he and his God won that day. My people gathered at other temples of Dagon and prayed for strength in our next encounter with the Israelites.

Lot's Wife

When the Lord destroyed the evil cities of Sodom and Gomorrah with fire and brimstone, we were a day's walk away—my father Lot, the nephew of Abraham, my mother, my sister, and me.

I still shudder when I think of that morning. Before sunrise the two men whom God had sent to us urged us to leave our home. "The Lord has sent us to destroy this wicked city," they told our father. "Before the sun sets this day, the entire valley and all the sinful people who dwell in it will be consumed by fire. So hurry, you and your family must leave this place at once."

My sister and I were both betrothed, and our father urged our husbands-to-be to go with us. But they thought our father was joking. They did not believe that disaster was going to rain from the sky, so they refused to leave

Sodom. My sister and I also found it incredible that such a frightful thing would occur. We wanted to stay in Sodom also. We were pleased when our mother and father delayed. "Perhaps we will not have to go after all," we comforted each other.

"Move again," our mother moaned. "I am tired of moving from place to place, being an outsider and having to make friends all over again." She clutched one of her delicately embroidered dowry cushions. "Must we give up all our possessions—our household goods and even our livestock? Where would we go?"

But the men of God persisted. "The Lord God is about to destroy this place," they insisted.

We could not imagine such a disaster as they were describing. Whole cities and towns destroyed!

But the messengers seized me and my sister and our parents by the hand and, ignoring our protests, brought us outside the city. They held our mother by the arms and spoke to her urgently. "Flee for your lives and do not stop until you are well out of the valley. See the hills there on the horizon? Flee there or you will be consumed by the mighty flames as they devour every living thing in the valley."

"But the hills are at least a day's journey away," our father protested. "What about that settlement to the west, the small one at the edge of the valley? It's close enough that we could reach it before dark."

"Yes," implored our mother, "let us go there. We would not survive the climb to the hills. Besides, we do not want to settle so far from our old home."

"Your old home will be flat ground. Scorched as though it had never risen as an abomination to the Lord God."

"I do not want to leave the home where we have been so happy." My mother wept bitterly.

Seeing her grief, the men agreed. "We will grant your

request. Go to that settlement, and we will spare it when we destroy everything else. Now go at once; we can do nothing until you are safely there. Only remember, whatever you do, do not turn around. Do not look behind you. For you must not look upon the destruction of Sodom and Gomorrah."

As fast as we were able, we made our way in the direction of the city. The sky was bloodred, and fire rained down from heaven in the direction of Sodom. "Don't look back." I held my sister close to me, shielding her eyes with my hand.

"Faster," our father urged our mother, "or God's anger will engulf us."

But our mother slowed her steps. "Our home," she sobbed, "and our friends. If only we did not have to leave them. If only I could see them again—"

She stopped. She wiped her eyes. She took one quick glance over her shoulder, and she was turned into a pillar of salt.

The Daughters of Zelophehad

The people of Israel had been living in the wilderness for many years. We, the five daughters of Zelophehad, were born long after Moses and Miriam and Aaron led our people out of the land of Egypt. We endured difficult times in the desert. Times of thirst and famine. Times of uncertainty and confusion. But the Lord our God guided us through the barren lands, and Moses taught us the laws that he learned from God on Mount Sinai.

We had been traveling for many years and now were living on the plains of Moab. Many of the elders have died, including our own mother. I, Mahlah, am of a marriageable age, and soon Noah and Milcah will be too. My sisters and I talk about some of the young men from our tribe, the family of Manasseh, the tribe of Joseph. Our father had been preparing to arrange a marriage for me, but then several days ago he died.

"What will we do, now that we are alone? Who will find husbands for each one of us?" my sister Noah wondered. Hoglah and Milcah wanted to go to Moses and seek the word of the Lord. But we thought of a story we had heard about Moses' sister Miriam, who had been punished by God for criticizing Moses. She had been struck with a skin disease and had to remain outside the camp for seven days until she had been healed. If Miriam had been punished for questioning the words of her brother Moses, what would happen to the five of us, who were neither prophets nor leaders to our people, but young orphans?

Since we had no one to speak for us, I agreed that we had to risk the anger of Moses, the elders, and the Lord. It did not seem just and fair that the name of our father should be lost to the family because there are no sons to inherit his portion. Although our littlest sister Tirzah was frightened at approaching the Tent of Meeting, where crowds of people were gathered, Milcah and I held her hands and pretended that we were not as frightened as she was!

Eliezer the priest and the leaders of the congregation were standing at the entrance to the Tent of Meeting. Behind them stood men and women from each of the twelve tribes. Moses held out his hands toward us. "What is it that you seek, daughters of Zelophehad?"

Suddenly appearing before the great leader himself, seeing his eyes burning in his lined and weathered face, we fell silent. Never before had I stood so close to this man who had spoken face-to-face with God. His beard was thick and grizzled; his hands were curled around his great staff that had led us to the next spring of fresh water for so many years. Could we dare ask him to change the law so that our father's name might live?

"Speak!" Eliezer said.

My sisters looked to me as the eldest. I stepped forward and concentrated on Moses' kindly expression. He was not much older than my own dear father had been. "As you know, my lord, my father was a good man. He was not among the wicked men who gathered together and spoke against the Lord in the company of Korah. As you know, he had no sons. Only the five of us. We ask that we be allowed to keep his inheritance, so that we may work the land of his estate, and our family may continue as though he had sons to inherit from him."

"Women inherit their father's land?" Eliezer seemed shocked. "Never in the forty years since we left Egypt has anyone suggested that we change the law."

Moses shook his head at Eliezer to silence him. "The Lord our God has given us the land, and it is for the Lord to decide through whose hands it shall pass. I shall inquire of the Lord, Mahlah, and tomorrow I shall tell you what God has decreed concerning your case."

The next day we went again to the door of the Tent of Meeting. Moses was waiting for us, along with the elders and Eliezer the priest. Moses stepped forward and addressed the people. "The Lord God has spoken. God has said that the daughters of Zelophehad are right to care for their father's estate. They shall possess their father's land.

And from now on, if any father dies and has no sons, then his inheritance shall pass to his daughters. But if they are married to sons from other tribes of our people, then their inheritance will be taken from the portion of their father and added to the general property of the tribe. This is the word of the Lord our God, and it shall be for us a law."

The elders nodded and Moses turned back to us. "You are brave women to protect the inheritance of your father. He would be proud of you this day. So long as you marry within your father's family, you shall inherit your father's portion and it shall pass to your sons."

"And if we have only daughters, it shall pass to them?" asked my sister Noah.

Moses and the elders laughed. "That is right. Within the land of Israel daughters will always be permitted to inherit the land of their fathers because the daughters of Zelophehad dared to question the law as it was and sought to change it."

For Further Reading

Bickerman, Elias. *Four Strange Books of the Bible.* Schocken, 1967.

Cansdale, George S. *All the Animals of the Bible Lands.* Zondervan, 1970.

Clines, David J. A. *The Esther Scroll: The Story of the Story.* JSOT Press, 1984.

Harper's Bible Atlas. Harper & Row, 1987.

Harper's Bible Commentary. Harper & Row, 1988.

Harper's Bible Dictionary. Harper & Row, 1985.

The Interpreter's Dictionary of the Bible. Abingdon, 4 vols., 1962; supplementary vol., 1976.

King, Philip J. *Amos, Hosea, Micah: An Archaeological Commentary.* Westminster, 1988.

McCarter, P. Kyle, Jr. *I Samuel.* Anchor Bible, vol. 8. Doubleday, 1980.

———. *II Samuel.* Anchor Bible, vol. 9. Doubleday, 1984.

Meyers, Carol. *Discovering Eve: Ancient Israelite Women in Context.* Oxford University Press, 1988.

Moore, Carey A. *Esther.* Anchor Bible, vol. 7B. Doubleday, 1971.

———. *Judith.* Anchor Bible, vol. 40. Doubleday, 1985.

Oxford Bible Atlas. Third edition. Oxford University Press, 1984.

Pritchard, J. B. *The Ancient Near East in Pictures.* Princeton University Press, 1954.

Sasson, Jack M. "Esther" and "Ruth" in *The Literary Guide to the Bible.* Belknap, 1987.

Seibert, Ilse. *Woman in the Ancient Near East.* Ed. Leipzig, 1974.

Zohary, Michael. *Plants of the Bible.* Cambridge University Press, 1982.

About the Authors

Alice Bach is an assistant professor of religious studies at Stanford University. She is the author of more than twenty books for children and young adults, including a series of picture books that have been translated into five languages. Two of her novels, *Waiting for Johnny Miracle* and *He Will Not Walk with Me,* have been ALA Notable Books. *Waiting for Johnny Miracle* was also chosen as a *New York Times* Best Book of the Year, as was *Molly Makebelieve.* She is the editor of *The Pleasure of Her Text: Feminist Readings of Biblical and Historical Texts.*

J. Cheryl Exum teaches Hebrew Bible at Boston College. She is the author of *Tragedy and Biblical Narrative: Arrows of the Almighty* (Cambridge University Press) and of numerous scholarly articles on biblical criticism and poetics. Her current project is a book about women in the Bible, entitled *Fragmented Women.*

This is their second collaboration for Delacorte Press. Their first was *Moses' Ark.*

About the Book

Miriam's Well was designed by Jane Byers Bierhorst. The text is set in Devinne roman, and the display type is Commercial Script and Devinne.

The frontispiece and decorations are by Leo and Diane Dillon. The frontispiece was done in acrylic, and the decorations in pen and ink.